COMBAT LEGEND

MITSUBISHI ZERO

Robert Jackson

Airlife

Copyright © 2003 The Crowood Press Ltd

First published in the UK in 2003
by Airlife Publishing, an imprint of The Crowood Press Ltd

Text written by Robert Jackson
Profile illustrations drawn by Dave Windle
Cover painting by Jim Brown – The Art of Aviation Co. Ltd

British Library Cataloguing-in-Publication Data
    A catalogue record for this book
    is available from the British Library

ISBN 1 84037 398 9

Printed in Malaysia

*Contact us for a free catalogue that describes the complete range of Airlife
books for pilots and aviation enthusiasts*

Airlife Publishing
An imprint of The Crowood Press Ltd
Ramsbury, Marlborough, Wiltshire SN8 2HR
E-mail: enquiries@crowood.com
Website: www.crowood.com

Contents

Zero Timeline

19 May 1937:
Preliminary specifications for a fighter to replace the Navy Type 96 Carrier Fighter (Mitsubishi A5M).

March 1939:
A6M1 Zero prototype completed.

1 April 1939:
Prototype A6M1 Zero makes its first flight at Kagamigahara with test pilot Katsuzo Shima at the controls.

28 December 1939:
Pre-production A6M2 Zero with Nakajima NK1C Sakae 12 engine begins flight trials.

21 July 1940:
15 A6M2s sent to the 12th Rengo Kokutai (12th Naval Air Corps) for combat evaluation in China.

13 September 1940:
Zeros score their first successes in China.

November 1940:
A6M2 Model 21, with folding wingtips, makes its appearance.

June 1941:
A6M3 with supercharged Sakae 21 engine and folding wingtips makes its appearance. Folding wingtips later removed and aircraft redesignated A6M3 Model 32.

September 1941:
A6M2s redeployed from China in readiness for offensive operations in the Pacific, having destroyed 99 Chinese aircraft.

7 December 1941:
328 A6M2s spearhead a two-pronged attack on American and Allied forces in Hawaii and the Philippines.

8 December 1941:
First flight of the Nakajima A6M-2 fighter floatplane version of the A6M2 Zero.

April 1942:
First appearance of the A6M2-N floatplane version of the Zero during the Solomons campaign. Attacks on Colombo and Trincomalee; attacks on Darwin.

May 1942:
Battle of the Coral Sea; attacks on Port Moresby, New Guinea.

May to June 1942:
Battles of Midway and the Coral Sea result in serious losses of Zero fighters and trained pilots when Japanese carriers are sunk.

August to November 1942:
A6M3 Zeros sustain heavy losses in the Battle of Guadalcanal.

May to June 1943:
Renewed attacks on Darwin; attacks on Russell Islands, Rendova (Solomons) and Brocks Creek.

August 1943:
Attacks on Vella Lavella (Solomons), Brocks Creek.

August 1943:
First appearance of an improved version of the Zero, the A6M5 (Navy Type 0 Carrier Fighter Model 52).

6 May 1944:
First flight of the Mitsubishi A7M *Reppu* (Hurricane), the Zero's intended successor.

June to July 1944:
Air defence operations, Iwo Jima.

June to November 1944:
Air operations over the Philippines.

25 October 1944:
First use of Zero fighters in the *kamikaze* suicide attack role, during the Battle of Leyte Gulf Philippines).

November 1944:
First appearance of the A6M6c Zero Model 53C with a water-methanol boosted Sakae 31 engine.

February 1945:
Air defence operations, Japan.

April 1945:
First of two A6M8 prototypes (Navy Type 0 Carrier Fighter Model 64) completed with Mitsubishi MK8P Kinsei 62 engine.

April 1945:
Kamikaze and escort missions off Okinawa.

May 1945:
First appearance of the A6M7 Model 63 Zero dive-bomber and *kamikaze* variant.

1. Mitsubishi Zero: Prototypes and Development

The path of evolution that led to the Mitsubishi Zero, one of the most remarkable fighter aircraft of all time, began in June 1912, when a Naval Aeronautical Research Committee was set up by the Imperial Japanese Navy. Soon afterwards, six selected officers were sent to France and the United States, with orders to purchase a number of seaplanes, which they were to learn to fly and maintain. In November that year, a small naval air base was established on the coast near Yokosuka, and in the months that followed a small number of naval officers received flight and technical training there.

In 1913, the Imperial Japanese Navy commissioned its first seaplane tender, the *Wakamiya Maru*, and in September and October 1914 four seaplanes operating from this vessel carried out bombing and reconnaissance operations against the German fortress of Tsingtao, on the Chinese coast. By the end of World War I two Naval Air Corps, the Yokosuka and Sasebo *Kokutai*s, had been activated, the first in April 1916 and the second in March 1918.

Deck take-off

The two years after the end of World War I saw little progress in Japanese naval aviation, although in June 1920 a Lt Kuwabara made the first successful take-off by a Japanese naval aviator from a deck mounted on the *Wakamiya Maru*; he was flying an imported Sopwith Pup. The impetus for further naval aviation development came in 1921, with the arrival in Japan of the British Aviation Mission, its aviation instructors being accompanied by aircraft that were modern for their time.

Meanwhile, construction had begun of the first Japanese aircraft carrier. She was later to be described as the world's first purpose-built carrier, but this is not quite true, as she was originally designed as an auxiliary tanker which had provision for carrying aircraft. Originally named *Hiryu* (Flying Dragon), she was laid down in October 1919. Renamed *Hosho* (Soaring Phoenix), the vessel was redesignated an aircraft depot ship in October 1921. *Hosho* was launched on 13 November that year and completed in December 1922.

The early 1920s saw the establishment of Kawasaki, Mitsubishi and Nakajima as the 'big three' of Japan's embryo aircraft industry, whose early development work relied heavily on aid from Britain, the USA, France and Germany. Japanese factories concentrated mainly in the licence production of foreign designs and on the overhaul of types purchased directly from abroad, such as the Gloster Sparrowhawk (a development of the Nieuport Nighthawk).

In 1923, the German Dr Richard Vogt (later of Blohm und Voss) became chief designer for Kawasaki, and he was responsible for designing a two-seat general-purpose biplane, the KDA-2, which entered service with the Imperial Japanese Army as the Type 88.

The Mitsubishi design team was led by Herbert Smith, formerly of the Sopwith company. The Mitsubishi B1M, the first

The Nakajima A2N (Type 90) naval fighter was developed from the Nakajima-built version of the British Gloster Gambet. A small unequal-span single-bay biplane, it had stylishly tapered wings with elliptical tips and considerable stagger. Ailerons were fitted on upper and lower wings. (*Philip Jarrett*)

Japanese aircraft designed for the torpedo attack role, appeared in 1922. It remained in production until 1933, by which time 442 had been produced for the Imperial Japanese Navy and 48 for the Army.

Type numbers

The B1M's replacement was the Mitsubishi B2M1, a metal structure torpedo-bomber-reconnaissance aircraft which was actually designed by Blackburn Aircraft Ltd as the Navy Type 89. The 'type numbers' of Japanese aircraft indicated the year in which the aircraft was manufactured according to the Japanese calendar, showing the last two digits. 'Type 89' meant that the B2M1 entered production in 1929, the Japanese year 2589.

Herbert Smith's team also designed the Mitsubishi 1MF, a carrier-borne biplane fighter, which in February 1923 made the first successful take-off by a Japanese-built aircraft from Japan's first aircraft carrier, the *Hosho*. Production of the 1MF ended in 1929, with the 138th machine.

In 1931 Nakajima produced the A2N carrier-borne fighter, which was developed from the Navy Type 3 Carrier Fighter. This was a version of the British-designed Gloster Gambet,

produced as a replacement for the Imperial Japanese Navy's ageing Sparrowhawks. An extremely agile biplane with stylishly tapered, staggered wings, the A2N was very popular with its pilots. It entered service in 1930 as the Navy Type 90 Carrier Fighter and production ended in 1936 with the 106th aircraft.

Nakajima A2Ns were used operationally in the Sino-Japanese war, operating from the carrier *Kaga* in the Shanghai area. The A2N's replacement was the Nakajima A4N1, which entered service as the Type 95 Carrier Fighter. It had been developed in response to a Japanese Navy requirement for an interim fighter, 221 being produced between 1935 and 1938. It, too, participated in the Sino-Japanese conflict, carrying out ground attack operations in addition to establishing air superiority.

Meanwhile, in 1934, the recently organized Naval Aircraft Establishment had initiated the so-called *9-Shi* programme. *9-Shi* was the 9th year of *Showa*, the reign of His Imperial Highness Hirohito, which was to result in the production of several famous Japanese warplanes. Among them was the Mitsubishi A5M Type 96 Carrier Fighter, designed by a team under the direction of an up-and-coming young engineer named Jiro Horikoshi.

Developed from the A2N, the Nakajima A4N1 (Type 95) naval fighter was the Imperial Japanese Navy's main fighter and ground attack aircraft during the first year of the Sino-Japanese conflict. It was essentially an interim aircraft, filling the gap until suitable monoplane types became available. *(Philip Jarrett)*

Horikoshi had already worked on a fighter design under an earlier *7-Shi* programme, which was a failure, but now he had latitude to implement his own ideas, and lost no time in putting them into practice.

Monoplane carrier fighter

First flown in prototype form in January 1935, the Mitsubishi A5M was Japan's first carrier-borne monoplane fighter and its appearance was of great importance, for it marked the end of Japanese dependence on foreign designs. The prototype had an inverted gull wing, but subsequent aircraft featured a wing with a straight centre section and dihedral on the outboard panels. Much attention was paid to streamlining, the metal skin of the airframe being flush-riveted and all skin crevices and other irregularities being filled and painted to a smooth finish. Every possible device was used in an effort to save weight.

The aircraft was powered by a 600-hp Nakajima Kotobuki 5 engine, with which it reached a maximum level flight speed during trials of 450 km/h (280 mph), which was nearly 100 km/h (60 mph) faster than its design specification speed.

The initial production model was designated A5M1 Type 96 and had an enclosed cockpit, the first to be used by a Japanese fighter. It was not popular with the A5M's pilots and subsequent variants reverted to an open cockpit. These were the A5M2a, with a more powerful engine, and the A5M2b, with a three-blade propeller. The A5M3 was an experimental model fitted with a 20-mm cannon firing through the propeller hub, and the last production model was the A5M4, the A5M4-K being a tandem two-seat trainer version.

There was some delay between the final approval of the A5M1 and its acceptance by the Imperial Japanese Navy, the choice of a suitable engine being the main obstacle. But in August 1937, during the conflict between Japan and China, six A5M1s were assigned to the aircraft carrier *Kaga*, and on 22 August two of them were flown to an airstrip near the front in Manchuria, making their first sortie that same day. On this occasion no contact was made with the enemy, but on 4 September two Type 96s, led by Lt Tadashi Nakajima, shot down three Curtiss Hawks.

On the 7th, three aircraft led by Lt Igarashi destroyed several Chinese aircraft, Igarashi claiming three of them. From then on the *Kaga*'s Type 96 fighter squadron was widely used in China, their opponents including Gloster Gladiators. In one air battle against 21 Gladiators, Hawks and other types, which took place on 30 August 1938, the *Kaga* fighter squadron claimed to have destroyed 11 enemy aircraft for the loss of two of its own number.

The A5M, later to be code-named 'Claude' by the Allies, saw very limited action in the Philippines at the onset of the Pacific war. About 1000 were built.

More range required

On 19 May 1937, preliminary specifications for a new Navy Experimental Carrier Fighter to replace the A5M were submitted to Mitsubishi and Nakajima under the *12-Shi* development programme. An analysis of the A5M's early combat performance in China, however, revealed a number of shortcomings, one of which was that the type had insufficient range

---

Mitsubishi A5M2
Crew: 1
Powerplant: one 785-hp Nakajima Kotobuki 41 9-cylinder radial
Max speed: 435 km/h (270 mph) at 3000 m (9845 ft)
Service ceiling: 9800 m (32,150 ft)
Max range: 1400 km (870 miles)
Wing span: 11.00 m (36 ft 1 in)
Length: 7.7 m (24 ft 9 in)
Height: 3.27 m (10 ft 8 in)
Weights: 1822 kg (4017 lb)
Armament: two fixed forward-firing 7.7-mm (0.303-in) machine-guns in upper forward fuselage; external bomb load of 60 kg (132 lb)

---

to escort Japanese bombers on deep-penetration missions to targets in mainland China.

The specification for the new *12-Shi* carrier fighter was therefore revised and made more stringent, not only because of the experience in China, but also because reports were reaching Japan of the new generation of fighter monoplanes under development in the west: the Messerschmitt Bf 109, the Hawker Hurricane and Supermarine Spitfire, and the Curtiss Hawk 75A.

The new specification, issued in October 1937, called for a fighter capable of intercepting and destroying enemy attack bombers, and of serving in the escort role with a performance better than that of enemy interceptors. Maximum speed was to be better than 500 km/h (311 mph) at 4000 m (13,123 ft) in level

The Mitsubishi A5M (Type 96) was Japan's first carrier-borne monoplane fighter. Its appearance marked the end of Japan's dependence on foreign designs. A great deal of attention was paid to streamlining, the metal skin of the airframe being flush-riveted. The type was later given the reporting name 'Claude' by the Allies. (*Philip Jarrett*)

The Imperial Japanese Army's equivalent of the Navy's A5M was the Nakajima Ki.27, the first Japanese aircraft to feature an enclosed cockpit. It was widely used in the Army's initial land offensives during World War II, particularly in Burma, and was given the Allied code-name 'Nate'. (*Philip Jarrett*)

flight, with the ability to climb to 3000 m (9843 ft) within 3 min 30 sec of leaving the ground (3 min 45 sec from start of take-off roll).

Endurance at 3000 m at normal power setting, fully loaded with auxiliary fuel tank, was to be between one and two hours, or up to eight hours at maximum range cruising speed. In fact, an endurance of 10 hours was attainable at 115 knots at 3660 m (12,000 ft) and a power setting of 1700 to 1850 rpm, reducing fuel consumption to 18 gallons per hour. The take-off run in still-air conditions was not to exceed 175 m (574 ft), reducing to 70 m (230 ft) with a 43 km/h (30 mph) head wind.

The armament was to be two 20-mm cannon and two 7.7-mm (0.303-in) machine-guns, and there was to be provision for the carriage of two 30-kg (66-lb) or 60-kg (132-lb) bombs.

Following a technical review held at the Naval Aircraft Establishment in Yokosuka on 17 January 1938, Nakajima decided that it was impossible to meet the demands of the revised specification, and withdrew from the competition. Mitsubishi elected to proceed, and Jiro Horikoshi set about organising a design team. Key personnel included Yoshitoshi Sone and Teruo Tojo, responsible for the theoretical calculations; Yoshio Toshikawa, assisted by Sone, for the structural work; Denichiro Inoue and Shotaro Tanaka for engine installation; Yoshimi Hatakenaka for the armament and auxiliary equipment (which included the oxygen system, engine fire extinguisher, lighting equipment and instruments); and Sadahiko Kao and Takeyoshi Moro for the landing gear and associated equipment.

Suitable engine

The design team's principal problem was to find a suitable engine around which to design the airframe. As there was at that time no suitable liquid-cooled in-line engine in Japan, three 14-cylinder radials were evaluated: the 875-hp Mitsubishi Zuisei 13, the 950-hp

Nakajima Sakae 12, and the 1070-hp Kinsei 46. The Nakajima engine was initially rejected as it was designed by a competitor, and it was the Kinsei that found favour with Horikoshi; but because of the Navy's insistence on a power loading not exceeding 5.5-lb/hp, the heavier and more powerful Kinsei was abandoned and the Zuisei 13 was selected to power the prototype.

Interestingly, Horikoshi never ceased lobbying for the adoption of the Kinsei; it was finally selected as the powerplant for the last Zero variant, the A6M8, but by that time the war was lost and only two prototype aircraft were completed.

A two-blade variable pitch propeller was fitted to the prototype, but this was replaced during the flight test phase by a constant speed three-blade Sumitomo-Hamilton propeller.

In order to meet the exacting Navy requirement, weight conservation was of paramount importance, and the 12-Shi design featured several innovations in order to achieve this goal. The wing was built in one piece, eliminating the need for the heavy centre-section fittings normally required for joining two separate wing sections. The one-piece wing combined with the engine, cockpit and forward fuselage to form a single rigid unit, the centre section of the fuselage being riveted to the upper wing skin, which formed the cockpit floor. The rear fuselage, with the tail, was joined to the forward section by a series of 80 bolts, fixed to two ring formers just aft of the cockpit. The aircraft could therefore readily be split into two components, facilitating storage and also providing unobstructed access to the cockpit area from the rear.

Special alloy

Another weight-saving device was the use of a lightweight alloy called Extra-Super Duralumin (ESD) in the construction of the wing main spar. Manufactured by Sumitomo Metal Industry, it had a tensile strength 30 to 40 per cent higher than any alloy used previously. Although very light in weight (1680 kg/3704 lb empty, compared with the Spitfire I's 1969 kg/4341 lb), a feature that gave the impression that the airframe was structurally weak, the 12-Shi fighter design was actually very strong.

Horikoshi and his design team had given a

great deal of thought to the 12-Shi fighter's aerodynamics. The aircraft was designed to produce the minimum of drag, while remaining inherently stable and easy to fly. Because of the requirement to reduce the wing loading to a figure less than 105 kg/m² (21.5 lb/sq ft) to produce optimum take-off, climb and manoeuvrability, the aircraft was given a wing area of 22.44 m² (241.54 sq ft), and a new aerofoil section was selected. This was the Mitsubishi 118, which offered minimal centre of pressure movement, an important factor in reducing drag.

Armament

The primary armament selected for the 12-Shi fighter was the licence-built 20-mm Oerlikon cannon. The Swiss design was used by a number of European fighter aircraft, including the French Dewoitine D.510. Japan acquired two of these aircraft for evaluation in 1935; results showed that although the Oerlikon had a low muzzle velocity, it was light and sufficiently compact to permit installation in an aerodynamically clean wing. A further advantage was that it fired explosive shells.

A new company, the Dai-Nihon Heiki Company Ltd (The Japan Munitions Company Ltd) was set up to mass-produce the weapon and its ammunition under licence as the Type 99 Standard Naval Aircraft Cannon. The early version used drum magazines, while the later Type 99 Model 2 Mk 4 was belt-fed. The weapon was constantly improved throughout the war, some 35,000 cannon being produced by half a dozen factories. In the 12-Shi fighter design, one Type 99 was installed in each wing just outboard of the landing gear, each gun having 60 rounds. The secondary armament comprised two Type 97 7.7-mm (0.303-in) machine-guns, installed in the upper forward fuselage above the engine and firing through the propeller arc.

The prototype 12-Shi Experimental Carrier-Borne Fighter was completed at Mitsubishi's Nagoya plant on 16 March 1939, and three days later, after completion of weight and balance calculations and preliminary engine runs, it was dismantled and shipped rather incongruously on two ox-drawn wagons to the Army flying field at Kagamigahara, about 40 km (25 miles) to the north. After reassembly,

A Mitsubishi A6M2 *Reisen* (Zero Fighter) of the 12th Air Group, seen over China shortly after the type's entry into service. The design team's main problem was to find a suitable engine for the new fighter. Three 14-cylinder radials were evaluated before the Nakajima Sakae was selected for production aircraft. (*Philip Jarrett*)

This photograph, of a captured A6M2 undergoing flight testing at San Diego in 1943, shows the fighter's clean, uncomplicated lines to good effect. Everything possible was done to save weight, including the use of a lightweight alloy called Extra-Super Duralumin or ESD. (*USAF*)

Picture of the first captured Zero, with undercarriage and flaps extended. This aircraft was rebuilt from the wreck of the Zero which crashed on Akutan island early in June 1942, killing its pilot, Petty Officer Tadayoshi Koga. The Zero was not discovered until five weeks later. (*USAF*)

Mitsubishi test pilot Katsuzo Shima carried out taxi trials and then, at 07.30 on 1 April, 1939, he took the aircraft on its first flight. In fact it was not a real flight at all, just a brief hop along the runway to test the control responses; the flight testing proper began the next day.

Apart from some necessary minor adjustments to the landing gear, no serious snags were encountered apart from a vibration problem, which was cured by fitting a three-blade constant speed propeller in place of the two-blade one.

On 14 September 1939, having met all the requirements, the aircraft was officially accepted by the Imperial Japanese Navy and given the designation A6M1 Type 0 Carrier-Borne Fighter. The alpha numeric designation was seldom used, the fighter being commonly known as the *Rei Shiki Sento Ki* (Type Zero Fighter), often abbreviated to *Rei-sen* or *Reisen*.

On 25 October 1939 the Navy took delivery of the second Zero prototype, which among other tasks undertook armament trials. The third prototype, which began flight trials on 28 December 1939, was powered by the Nakajima NK1C Sakae 12 engine, common sense having at last prevailed over inter-company rivalry.

This was to become the first production model of the Zero. Designated A6M2, it was to provide the backbone of the Imperial Japanese Navy's fighter force during the first half of the Pacific War.

On 11 March 1940, the second prototype was carrying out a series of dives to investigate an engine overspeeding problem at Oppama field when it disintegrated, killing its pilot, Lt Shimokawa. Shimokawa was actually thrown clear and his parachute deployed, but he slipped from his harness and fell into the sea. He may have been unconscious, or already dead. The cause was never fully established, although the chief suspect was elevator flutter after failure of the mass balance; this would have created severe vibration, imposing intolerable stresses on the airframe.

China deployment

Despite this setback production continued, the first A6M2s being assigned to the Yokosuka Air Group Fighter Squadron after completing their production flight test schedule at the Naval Air Technology Arsenal. The Air Group's task was to bring the new fighter into full operational squadron service, flying the aircraft to its limits

An A6M2 Model 21 Zero of the 3rd Naval Air Group, bearing the serial X-182. The photograph was taken early in 1942, when the group was based on Rabaul for operations in the Dutch East Indies. The bands on fuselage and tail denote that the aircraft is used by a commanding officer. (*Philip Jarrett*)

and developing combat tactics to suit its superior performance.

Navy pilots were keen to assess the Zero's performance under actual combat conditions, and in July 1940 approval was granted for a number of aircraft to be deployed to China for combat trials with the 12th Air Group Fighter Squadron – much to the dismay of the Mitsubishi engineering team, who considered that there were still some modifications to be made before the Zero could be cleared for combat. Their objections were overruled, and on 21 July an advance unit of six Zeros under the command of Lt Tamotsu Yokoyama deployed to the city of Wuhan, to be followed by nine more aircraft at intervals.

On 19 August, Yokoyama led 12 Zeros on a mission to escort 54 Mitsubishi G3M2 bombers (later to receive the Allied code-name 'Nell') in an attack on Hankow. No enemy fighters rose to challenge the raiders, and the fighter pilots returned to base without having fired a shot.

Another escort mission, this time involving an attack on Chungking by 27 bombers, was flown on 12 September. Despite the fact that post-raid reconnaissance revealed the presence of over 30 enemy fighters at dispersed locations around the city, none offered any opposition, so the Zero pilots carried out strafing attacks on Shihmachow airfield and other targets of opportunity on the ground as the bombers left the target area.

First air battles

The next day, 13 September, was a very different story. The target was again Chungking, and this time the bombers were escorted by 13 Zeros led by Lt Saburo Shindo. At first, it seemed as though this mission would be a repetition of the earlier one, for no enemy fighters put in an appearance during the raid. As the bombers and their escort turned for home, however, a Japanese reconnaissance aircraft cruising high above Chungking

The Zero's primary task in its first combat missions over China was to escort bombers. The Mitsubishi G3M bomber, later to be assigned the Allied code-name 'Nell', was widely used for strategic bombing in China. It was also used for long-range reconnaissance missions, photographing targets in the Philippines and elsewhere prior to the Japanese offensive in the Pacific. Note the external bomb racks. (*Philip Jarrett*)

reported that about 30 enemy fighters were assembling over the target area, apparently getting ready to pursue and attack the retreating bombers.

Shindo at once ordered his fighters to turn back towards Chungking, climbing hard as they did so. The Chinese fighters – Polikarpov I-15 biplanes and I-16 monoplanes – were taken completely by surprise, and the air battle that followed was one-sided in the extreme. No fewer than 27 of the enemy aircraft were destroyed, either shot down or damaged to such an extent that they crashed while attempting to land.

Ace in a day

One of Shindo's pilots, Warrant Officer Koshiro Yamashita, became an ace by destroying five enemy aircraft that day; Petty Officer 2nd Class Yoshio Oki got four; PO 1st Class Tora-ichi Takatsuka shot down three; six other pilots destroyed two each, while five – one of whom was Shindo – claimed one each. It was a resounding success for the Japanese and for the

Zero fighter; it was widely publicised in Japan – and it passed completely unnoticed in the west.

The appearance of the Zero came as an unpleasant shock to the Chinese. Their pilots, poorly trained to start with, looked upon the Japanese fighter with almost superstitious awe, regarding it as invincible. On 16 September 1940, three days after the Chungking battle, six Zeros pounced on a large, unidentified Chinese aircraft in the same area and shot it down. This was the last mission flown in September, the Zeros being temporarily withdrawn for inspection and overhaul in preparation for missions that would taken them still deeper into Chinese territory.

It is worth noting that the Japanese were a long way ahead of everyone else in the use of long-range fuel tanks. They were part of the Zero's standard equipment at the same time as the *Luftwaffe*'s Messerschmitt Bf 109 fighters, with no such capability, were constantly hampered by lack of endurance on their bomber escort missions over England.

Operational flying resumed on 4 October

One type frequently encountered by the Zero during operations in China was the Curtiss Hawk, seen here in Finnish Air Force markings. More Hawks were destroyed in accidents than by enemy action, as Chinese pilots were notoriously inept. On one occasion, six out of 13 Hawks crashed while attempting to land. (*Philip Jarrett*)

1940, when eight Zeros accompanied 27 bombers on a very long-range mission to Chengtsu, in the extreme west of Szechwan Province. No defending fighters were encountered, but after leaving the target area the Zero pilots made a surprise attack on Taipingssu airfield, shooting down five I-16s and a Tupolev SB-2 medium bomber that were in the vicinity before strafing the airfield itself. Air reconnaissance subsequently confirmed that at least 19 enemy aircraft had been destroyed on the ground.

Total supremacy
The Zero fighter quickly established total Japanese air supremacy in the China theatre, enabling the bombers to fly deep-penetration missions with virtual impunity, their crews secure in the knowledge that the Zero escorts were more than capable of dealing with anything the enemy might put up against them. Between 19 August 1940 and the end of the year, the Zeros flew 153 individual sorties in the course of 22 missions, destroying

59 Chinese aircraft in air combat and 101 on the ground for no loss to themselves.

In October 1940 the Mitsubishi G3M2 bomber force was withdrawn from operations in China to be reorganized and re-equipped, as it had suffered considerable losses prior to the arrival of the Zeros. For the next six months, until the bombers returned to China in April 1941, the Zeros conducted the air war virtually single-handed, and they had sufficient combat radius to attack the Chinese on all fronts. Between 1 January and 1 September 1941, the Zeros flew 354 sorties, in the course of which they destroyed 44 enemy aircraft and damaged 62 more for the loss of two of their own number, both brought down by anti-aircraft fire. The 12th Air Group disbanded in September 1941, most of its pilots being transferred to the Tainan Air Group or to the 3rd Air Group.

The 12th Air Group was not the only Zero unit to see combat in China in the months before the Pacific War. On 14 July 1940, the 14th Air Group Fighter Squadron, which had been

A captured Mitsubishi A6M2 Zero is seen in flight over San Diego. The aircraft was painted in US Navy blue-grey camouflage. Evaluating the Zero against Allied fighters dispelled the myth of the Japanese fighter's invincibility; certainly it was good, but the main fault was that American tactics were wrong. (*Philip Jarrett*)

supporting ground attack operations in South China, moved to Hanoi in French Indo-China, the northern part of which had been occupied by Japanese forces following France's defeat by Germany in the previous month.

As well as Type 96 aircraft, the fighter element of this formation included nine Zeros, and on the day of their arrival at Hanoi seven were detailed to escort 27 ground attack aircraft of the 15th Air Group in an attack on Kunming, in south-western China.

Over the target, the Japanese raiders were intercepted by a number of I-15, I-16 and Curtiss Hawk fighters; in an air battle lasting 15 minutes, 13 of them were shot down by the Zeros. Four enemy aircraft were also destroyed on the ground. And on 12 December, seven Zeros, with Army reconnaissance aircraft leading the way, flew the 547 km (340 miles) to Siangyun airfield and destroyed 22 Chinese aircraft in strafing attacks.

The 3rd Air Group, which was destined to become one of the most distinguished naval fighter units of the Pacific War, also operated out of Hanoi in the summer of 1941. Apart from some reconnaissance aircraft, it was an all-fighter formation; this was unique among Japanese air groups, which were normally composed of a mixture of fighters, army cooperation and bomber aircraft. Many of its pilots had been transferred from the 12th Air Group, and were among the most experienced in the world. Even the newest pilots had around 1000 hours' flying time to their credit.

Based on Formosa

By October 1941, when the main force moved to Takao on Formosa (Taiwan), the 3rd Air Group's strength stood at 45 A6M2 Zero Type 21 and 12 A5M Type 96 aircraft. Thirteen more Zeros remained in southern Indo-China to take part in the forthcoming campaign in Malaya.

Because of an almost complete lack of intelligence, identifying Japanese combat aircraft called for much guesswork by Allied air forces. The A6M2 Zero was code-named 'Zeke', and was described as such in most combat reports. The name 'Zero' did not come into general usage until later in the war. (*Philip Jarrett*)

The Taiwan-based elements of the group underwent a period of intensive training from mid-October 1941, in preparation for the assault on the Philippines. The training emphasised flying for range and endurance. With a 1930 km (1200 mile) round trip involved, the original plan was for the Zeros to land on a carrier at the midway point and refuel before continuing. However, with experience, the pilots became so confident in the Zero's long-range capability that they planned to fly non-stop to the Philippines and back, with 20 minutes of combat patrol time included.

Similar training was also carried out by another Taiwan-based formation, the Tainan Air Group, which was to become the best known of all naval air groups and which was to have the largest number of aces. Formed at Tainan on 1 October 1941, the Group formed part of the 23rd Air Flotilla and, like the 3rd Group, had an establishment of 45 Zeros and 12 A5Ms. Fourteen of its Zeros were attached to the 22nd Air Flotilla in Indo-China, for operations in Malaya and the Dutch East Indies. Taking into account the 3rd Air Group fighters, the 22nd Air Flotilla had 26 Zeros at its disposal, plus some Type 96s, and on 1 December 1941 these were moved forward to Saigon in southern Indo-China.

By this time, the majority of the Imperial Japanese Navy's first-line fighter squadrons had been reequipped with the Zero. In the vanguard were the fighter units of the Navy's 1st Carrier Division, whose fast attack carriers, from April 1941, were assigned to the newly formed 1st Air Fleet. Its flagship was the large fleet carrier *Akagi*, whose air group included 16 Zeros with four reserves.

The other fleet carriers in service were the *Kaga* (18 Zeros with six reserves); *Soryu* (16 Zeros with four reserves); and *Hiryu* (16 Zeros with four reserves). By September, two more large carriers, the *Shokaku* and *Zuikaku*, had joined the fleet; both carried 12 Zero fighters, plus four spares. The light carrier *Ryujo*, on the other hand, retained her Mitsubishi A5M Type 96 fighters, forming part of the 4th Carrier Division alongside another small carrier, the *Kasuga Maru*.

On 6 December 1941, the day of the attack on Pearl Harbor (by Japanese time), the Imperial Japanese Navy had 521 fighters on strength, of which 328 were A6M2 Zeros. Within 48 hours, as they encountered this formidable fighter in action for the first time, the Americans and their allies in the Pacific and South-East Asia would be left in no doubt about the task that confronted them.

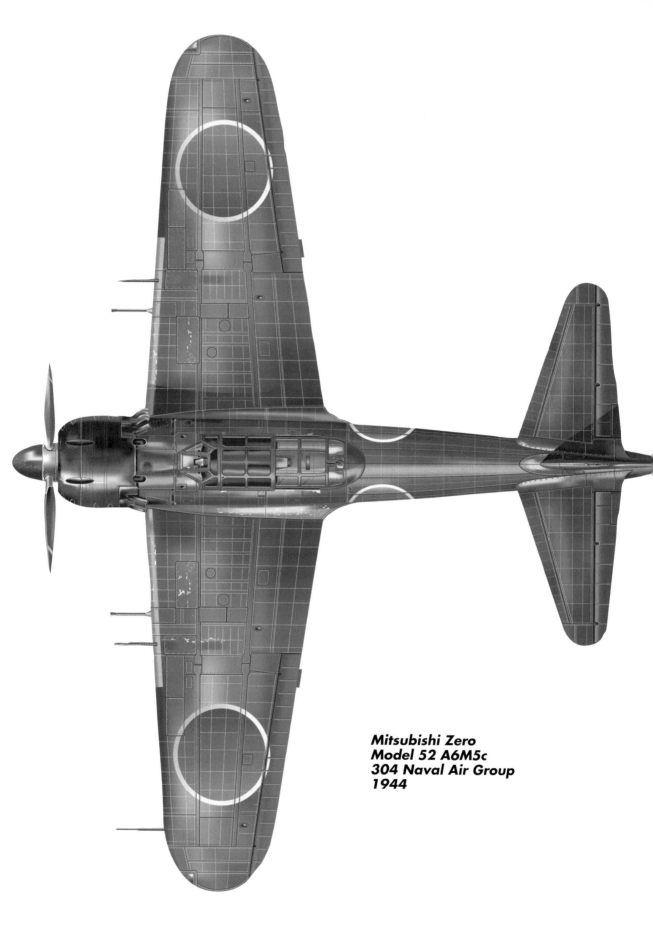

Mitsubishi Zero
Model 52 A6M5c
304 Naval Air Group
1944

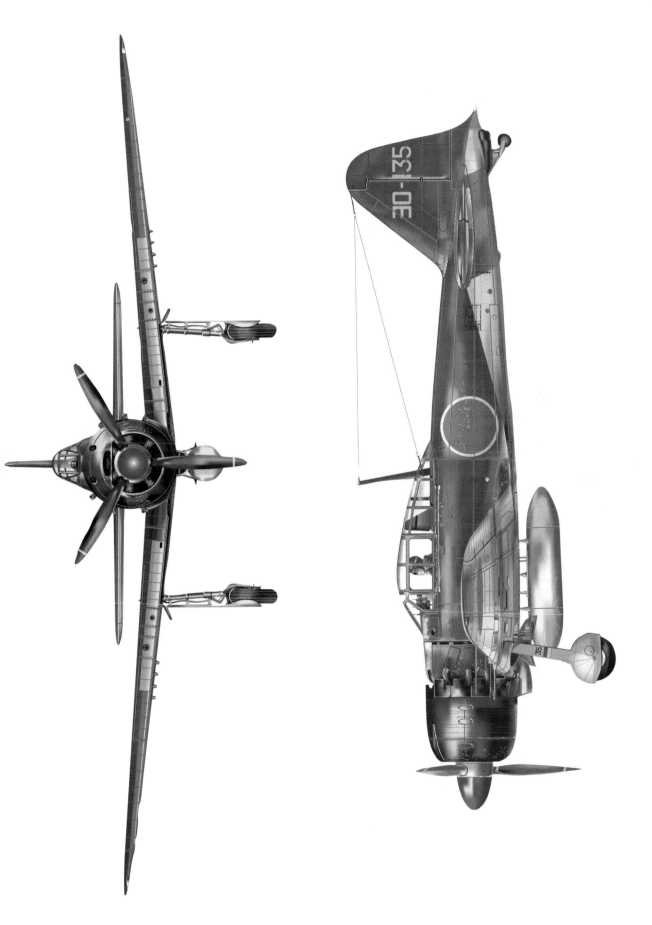

By the time Japan's carriers set off on the operation to attack the USA, the A6M2 provided the bulk of the IJN's seaborne fighter strength. Here, *Reisen* fighters of the *Shokaku*'s squadron prepare to launch on the morning of 7 December 1941. Their targets include Pearl Harbor and air bases all over Oahu. (*via Chris Bishop*)

A Mitsubishi Zero starts its take-off roll from the deck of the *Akagi*, flagship of the 1st Air Fleet. The primary mission for the fighters was to escort the Aichi D3A 'Val' dive-bombers and the Nakajima B5N 'Kate' torpedo-bombers as they attacked the US Navy's fleet anchorage at Pearl Harbor. (*via Chris Bishop*)

2. Zero in Action: Operational History

Final preparations for the Japanese attack on Pearl Harbor began on 22 November, 1941. The carriers of the 1st Air Fleet (*Akagi, Kaga, Hiryu, Soryu, Zuikaku* and *Shokaku*) assembled in Hitokappu Bay on Etoforu Island under the command of Vice-Admiral Chuichi Nagumo. They were accompanied by the battleships *Hiei* and *Kirishima*, the heavy cruisers *Tone* and *Chikuma*, the light cruiser *Abukuma* and nine destroyers of the 1st Destroyer Squadron.

The fleet sailed on 26 November, still prepared to turn back if diplomatic negotiations between Japan and the United States reached a satisfactory conclusion. They did not, and the coded signal *Niitaka Yama Nobore* (Climb Mount Niitaka), signifying that the Hawaiian operation was to go ahead, was transmitted to Vice-Admiral Nagumo on 2 December. After replenishment at sea, the fleet proceeded to its flying-off position 370 km (200 nautical miles) north of Oahu.

First wave

The first attack wave began leaving the carriers at 06.00 hours on 7 December, Hawaii time. It was escorted by 43 Zero fighters of the first wave covering force under Lt-Cdr Shigeru Itaya, officer commanding the *Akagi* Fighter Squadron. Itaya's Zeros arrived over Pearl Harbor at 07.50 Honolulu time; after shooting down a light aircraft and three trainers, they strafed Hickam and Ewa airfields, counting some 25 US aircraft burning on the ground. Itaya's wingman, PO 1st Class Takashi Hirano, was shot down by American anti-aircraft fire.

Six Zeros from the *Shokaku* and six from the *Zuikaku* strafed Kaneohe and Bellows Fields, setting on fire 33 aircraft, many of them PBY amphibians. These two carriers did not take part in the second-wave attack on Pearl Harbor, their fighters instead flying combat air patrols (CAP) over the fleet in relays.

During the second attack, nine Zeros from the *Akagi* led by the highly experienced Lt Saburo Shindo were detailed to escort 18 Aichi Type 99 (Val) dive-bombers. Arriving over the target about an hour after the first wave, and finding no opposition, the Zeros strafed Hickam Field, but only succeeded in destroying two aircraft on the ground.

The carrier *Kaga* despatched nine Zeros under Lt Nikaido, shooting down one aircraft and destroying about 20 more on the ground, but four of her Zeros were shot down by US fighters; it was the worst loss sustained by any of the carrier fighter squadrons.

Nine Zeros from the *Soryu* under Lt Fusato Iida also encountered strong opposition from American fighters during the second attack. Iida himself was shot down and killed in a strafing attack on Kaneohe, in which six PBYs were destroyed; Lt (Jg) Iyozo Fujita took over and was leading the flight away from the target area when they were intercepted. The Japanese pilots claimed two US fighters, but lost two of their own in the action.

Eight Zeros from the *Hiryu* strafed Kaneohe and Bellows Fields, claiming two aircraft and a truck before becoming involved in an air battle

Japanese intelligence on the dispositions of the US warships in Pearl Harbor was excellent, thanks to information provided by an extensive network of spies. Prior to the attack, the Japanese built a huge scale model of the entire American naval base, so that pilots knew exactly what to expect. (*USN*)

with US fighters, two of which were shot down by PO 1st Class Tsugio Matsuyama. One Zero pilot, PO 1st Class Shigenori Nishikaichi, made a forced landing on the Hawaiian island of Niihau, and was killed by a Hawaiian. In all, the Zero squadrons lost 15 aircraft out of a total of 79 deployed during the Hawaiian operation. There were 384 US aircraft on the islands: 188 were destroyed and another 159 damaged. Eighteen of the 94 US warships in Pearl Harbor were sunk or suffered major damage; eight of those were battleships.

Striking south

On 8 December 1941, the long hours of training carried out by the Taiwan-based air groups was at last put into practice when 51 Zeros of the

3rd Air Group and 44 of the Tainan Air Group made the long over-water flight to attack Iba and Clark airfields on Luzon, in the Philippines. Numerous American aircraft were destroyed on the ground, and about 19 in air combat. The 3rd Air Group lost two Zeros and the Tainan Air Group one, plus four that disappeared on the homeward flight.

On the 10th, the two Groups were involved in a major air battle near Manila, claiming 44 Allied aircraft destroyed and 42 damaged. Attacks on airfields in the vicinity of Manila were repeated on the next three days, but there was hardly any opposition and it was clear that the Allied air forces in the Philippines had been virtually wiped out.

On 14 December, a flight of the Tainan Air

Pearl Harbor under attack on the morning of Sunday, 7 December 1941. An Aichi 99 'Val' dive-bomber can be seen climbing away from 'Battleship Row' as the first bombs go down. By the end of the morning, many of the most powerful units of the US Pacific Fleet had been destroyed or badly damaged. (*USN*)

Group moved into Legaspi airfield in the Philippines, newly captured by Japanese forces, and continued to provide cover for the ground forces until late September, when the whole Group of 41 Zeros was ordered to deploy to the remote island of Horo. The move was completed by 7 January 1942, by which time the Group had begun attacks on the island of Tarakan, Borneo, in preparation for an amphibious assault. By 11 January the island had been captured, and the Group began its move forward on the 16th.

Meanwhile, the 3rd Air Group had moved up to Davao, Mindanao, on 23 December 1941, from where it was also able to conduct operations over Tarakan. On the 28th, seven Zero fighters engaged nine Dutch Brewster Buffalo fighters, destroying almost all of them. On 12 January, the 3rd Air Group began moving up to Kendari, in the Celebes, which had been overrun, and flew attack missions to Kupang, on Timor.

Borneo landings

On 24 January 1942 the Tainan Air Group provided cover from its Tarakan base for Japanese Army landings at Balikpapan, Borneo. In the course of these operations the Zero pilots encountered a variety of Allied bombers, including the Boeing B-17 Flying Fortress, whose heavy defensive firepower caused problems. However, in a battle over the Java Sea on 8 February, two B-17s were shot down by the use of head-on attacks.

In the meantime, the whole of the Tainan Group had moved to Balikpapan, where it was joined by the 3rd Air Group on 2 February. Both Groups were now well placed to conduct air superiority operations over eastern Java, and in the days that followed Allied aircraft fell in large numbers to the guns of the Zeros. On 3 February, 27 Zeros of the 3rd Air Group and 27 of the Tainan Air Group engaged in a major air battle with American and Dutch air units over Soerabaya. The Allies lost 39 aircraft in air combat and a further 21 on the ground. Altogether, around 90 Allied aircraft were destroyed on that day, giving the Japanese almost complete air superiority over Java.

Allied fighters encountered by the Zeros included RAF Hawker Hurricanes, evacuated to Java from Sumatra; Curtiss P-40 Tomahawks; Brewster Buffaloes; Curtiss Hawk 75As; and Curtiss-Wright CW-21B and CW-22s.

By 3 March 1942 the battle for Java was over, and on that day the 3rd Air Group, moving up to Kupang, sent out 17 Zero fighters under the command of Lt Miyano to attack the towns of Broome and Wyndham, in north-western Australia. The Zeros strafed a number of flying boats at their moorings and set them ablaze.

Devastation at Kaneohe Naval Air Station after the Japanese attack. There had been warnings of the assault, and a radar station had even detected the first of the incoming Japanese formations, but the warnings had been ignored or misinterpreted. The Americans were taken completely by surprise. (*USN*)

With its superb handling qualities, the Zero proved itself superior to any Allied aircraft that it encountered during the early Japanese campaigns in the Pacific. Apart from its flying attributes, every aspect of engine and airframe was designed for ease of access. (*Philip Jarrett*)

The 3rd Group had now been divided, part returning to Japan. The primary task of the remainder was to provide escorts for bombers attacking Darwin, where the main opposition consisted of the Curtiss P-40s of the USAAF's 49th Pursuit Group.

In April, the Tainan Air Group was deployed to Rabaul (New Britain), from where its main echelon of 24 Zeros moved up to Lae in eastern New Guinea for operations against the vital Allied base of Port Moresby. In the four-month period from April to July the Zeros claimed to have destroyed 201 Allied aircraft in air combat, with a further 45 probably destroyed, in the Port Moresby area alone, for the loss of only 20 Japanese fighters. The majority of the Allied fighters encountered during this phase were Bell P-39 Airacobras, which were no match at all for the Zero. During the early weeks of 1942 Zeros also provided escorts for bombers attacking Singapore and Rangoon.

Indian Ocean raid

Returning to their home base to rest and replenish following the Pearl Harbor attack, the Japanese aircraft carriers of the 1st Air Fleet sortied again in January 1942, proceeding independently to support Japanese amphibious operations in the Pacific. *Akagi*'s air group attacked Rabaul and other targets in the Bismarck Archipelago, and in February participated in the air raids on Port Darwin, her Zeros shooting down four Allied aircraft on the 19th and destroying eight more on the ground.

Kaga and *Soryu* also took part in these operations. The *Hiryu*, meanwhile, had been detached to support the assault on Wake Island; her air group took some losses during this operation, and she returned to Japan to make good the damage. *Shokaku* and *Zuikaku*, their fighter element now increased to 21 Zeros, also supported amphibious operations during January 1942.

Early in April 1942, the carriers *Akagi*, *Soryu*, *Hiryu*, *Zuikaku* and *Shokaku* made a sudden thrust into the Indian Ocean, the intention being to mount a heavy attack on British naval and air bases on Ceylon. On 5 April, the Japanese launched a strike of 52 Nakajima B5N 'Kate' high-level bombers and 38 Aichi D3A 'Val' dive-bombers, escorted by 36 Zeros, to attack Colombo. Fierce air battles developed over the city and harbour as the raiding force was intercepted by 42 Hurricanes and Fulmars; seven Japanese aircraft were destroyed, but 19 British fighters were shot down.

One of the first Allied types to fall foul of the Zero was the Brewster Buffalo. Although rejected by the RAF for service in Europe, it was considered good enough for the Far East. RAF, RAAF and RNZAF Buffaloes fought a hopeless battle against the Zero in the defence of Malaya and Singapore. It was used briefly by the Americans at Pearl Harbor and at Midway, and it featured in the defence of the Dutch East Indies, where it was operated by the Netherlands East Indies Army Air Corps. (*Philip Jarrett*)

In a second attack four days later, on the naval base at Trincomalee, nine out of a defending force of 23 British fighters were shot down. Five Bristol Blenheim medium bombers attempting to attack the carrier force were also shot down by the Zero CAP. Two of *Zuikaku's* Zeros were lost. The raids on Ceylon underlined, in almost contemptuous fashion, Japan's air superiority in the early months of 1942; but the situation was about to alter.

The Zero retained its overall ascendency during the first two years of the Pacific conflict, even though the Japanese suffered some serious reverses during this period. The first of these was the Battle of the Coral Sea in May 1942, when – in the first naval engagement in history fought without the opposing fleets making visual contact – American carrier forces prevented the Japanese from carrying out their proposed landing at Port Moresby, even though American losses were higher than those of their adversary. The Japanese carriers participating in this action were the *Shokaku*, *Zuikaku* and the light carrier *Shoho*, of the 5th Carrier Division. During the battle, which took place on 7 and 8 May, *Shoho*, which carried a mixed fighter complement of Zeros and A5Ms, was sunk and the *Shokaku* damaged by bomb hits; the Americans lost the carrier *Lexington*, while the *Yorktown* was damaged.

The *Shokaku* might well have been sunk had it not been for the action of a Zero pilot, PO 2nd Class Takeo Miyazawa, who deliberately rammed an American torpedo-bomber moments before it released its torpedo. The damaged *Shokaku* entered the port of Kure on 17 May for repairs.

In June came the decisive Battle of Midway,

The Curtiss P-40 was another American type that held the line with limited success against the Zero. It was used by the American Volunteer Group in China before Pearl Harbor. P-40s of the USAAF's 49th Fighter Group defended Darwin, and were employed by both the USAAF and the RAAF in New Guinea. (*Philip Jarrett*)

in which US Navy carrier dive-bombers smashed a strong Japanese force threatening Midway Island, the easternmost extremity of the Hawaiian chain.

Sailing for Midway

The Midway attack force, comprising the aircraft carriers *Akagi*, *Kaga*, *Soryu* and *Hiryu*, sailed from their base in Japan's inland sea on 27 May 1942. The task force was sighted by a PBY Catalina on 3 June. Six of the new TBF Avenger torpedo-bombers of VT-8's shore-based detachment were launched to attack the Japanese, together with Army B-17s and Marine SB2U Vindicators. None of the Avengers scored a hit and only one returned to Midway.

At 07.00 on 4 June the US carriers *Enterprise* and *Hornet* launched their strike groups, 14 TBDs (Douglas Devastators) of VT-6 and 15 of VT-8, with Grumman F4Fs of VF-6 flying top cover. VT-8 attacked first and all 15 aircraft were shot down by Zeros; only one crew

member survived. VT-6, attacking the *Kaga*, lost ten aircraft before they even reached their dropping points.

The *Enterprise*'s air group, attacking the *Soryu* with 12 TBDs of VT-3 and 17 SBDs (Douglas Dauntlesses) of VB-3, fared no better. Only five TBDs survived to make their torpedo attacks, and three of these were shot down on the way out. Of the 41 TBDs launched, only six returned to the task force, and one of these ran out of fuel and ditched.

But the sacrifice of the three torpedo-bomber squadrons was not in vain; they had absorbed the bulk of the Japanese fighter attacks, and had drawn the Zero cover down to sea level when 37 high-flying SBD Dauntless dive-bombers from the *Enterprise*'s VB-5 and 17 from *Yorktown*'s VB-3 made their attack, sinking the *Akagi*, *Kaga* and *Soryu*. The cost was 16 SBDs from the *Enterprise* air group.

A Japanese counter-attack from the *Hiryu* damaged the *Yorktown*, but the American

27

Although somewhat cramped by western standards, the Zero's 'birdcage' cockpit provided the pilot with a good all-round view. As a weight-saving measure, the Zero did not carry radio-telephony equipment, the pilots using hand signals instead. (*Philip Jarrett*)

carrier returned to full operation after a short time. Then a second attack was made by six Japanese torpedo-bombers; two were shot down, but the other four launched their torpedoes and two hit the carrier, which had to be abandoned. The hulk was later sunk by a submarine. At 17.00, the *Hiryu* was crippled in an attack by 24 SBDs from the *Enterprise*; the burned-out hulk was sunk by a Japanese destroyer the next day.

For the cost of 92 aircraft and the *Yorktown*, the US Navy had destroyed four fleet carriers, three quarters of the Japanese Navy's carrier striking force. With control of the air irretrievably lost, the Japanese withdrew under attack by Midway- and carrier-based aircraft.

Other US losses in the Midway battle included 40 shore-based aircraft. In addition to the four carriers, the Japanese lost one heavy cruiser and 258 aircraft. Though some aircrews were saved by destroyers, a large percentage of Japan's most experienced carrier pilots died.

It was a decisive defeat that effectively turned the tide of the Pacific war, as noted by a Japanese history of the battle:

'Special note should be taken of the activities of the *Hiryu* fighter squadron during the Battle of Midway. Nine carrier fighters under the command of Lt Shigematsu joined the first wave attack; they shot down a total of 18 F4Fs and Buffaloes that rose to intercept them. The unit itself returned safely to the carrier. The three aircraft carriers *Akagi*, *Kaga*, and *Soryu*, however, received hits from attacking American carrier aircraft and were destroyed by fire.

'The remaining carrier, the *Hiryu*, was able to send out two waves of attack forces by herself. This force severely damaged the carrier *Yorktown* – but not without cost. Casualties among the *Hiryu*'s aircraft were not minor.

'Six carrier fighters served as escort for the Kobayashi carrier bombing squadron, with the exception of two aircraft of the *Minegishi Chotai* that had to return prematurely to the carrier.

The Grumman F4F Wildcat was the standard US Navy and Marine fighter at the outbreak of the Pacific war. Although it suffered serious losses in combat with the Zero, in capable hands and using the right tactics it was a vital factor in helping to check the Japanese advance, especially at Guadalcanal. (*Philip Jarrett*)

The remaining four aircraft shot down seven enemy aircraft during an aerial encounter over the American task force. Our side suffered the loss of three aircraft also; Lt Shigematsu was the sole survivor who returned to the carrier.

'Four carrier fighters led by Lt Mori and reinforced by two carrier fighters from the *Kaga* escorted the Tomonaga torpedo attack squadron and participated in the attack on the American task force. After battling in the air with about 30 American fighters, the unit was able to shoot down 11 of the enemy; however, two aircraft, including the one piloted by Lt Mori, were destroyed. On the other hand, to provide combat air patrol directly over the carrier itself, a total of 33 aircraft were used, including planes that had been sent to the *Hiryu* from other carriers.

'Squadron wiped out'

'By evening and the tenth watch, a cumulative total of 33 enemy aircraft had been shot down. At the same time, five *Hiryu*-based fighters among others were also lost. As a matter of fact, the entire fighter squadron (aircraft) complement was wiped out. Also, the carrier *Hiryu* itself received bomb hits during the afternoon raids conducted on her, caught on fire, and sank the next morning. The Battle of Midway was a crushing defeat for Japan.'

The end of May 1942 found the carriers *Shokaku* and *Zuikaku* back in Japan, the former undergoing repairs at Kure and the latter in the inland sea. On 14 July a new task force, the 3rd Fleet, was organized around the destroyed 1st Carrier Division, absorbing its surviving pilots. The 1st Carrier Division, as reconstituted, now comprised the carriers *Shokaku*, *Zuikaku* and *Zuiho*. The *Zuiho* had originally been laid down as a submarine tender, the *Takasaki*, but was completed as a carrier and renamed. The fighter element of the *Shokaku* and *Zuikaku* now comprised 27 Zeros; that of the *Zuiho* 21.

On 16 August 1942, while the *Zuiho* was still fitting out, the *Shokaku* and *Zuikaku* sailed from the inland sea for the Solomons, where the Americans had landed and the fierce battle for the island of Guadalcanal had begun.

Also involved in these operations, on temporary attachment to the 3rd Fleet, was the light carrier *Ryujo*, which had been deployed to the Indian Ocean earlier in the year and whose aircraft had later taken part in attacks on the Aleutian Islands as a diversionary tactic at the time of the Midway battle. She had operated

The Bell P-39 Airacobra, although quite a capable aircraft at low level in the hands of a good pilot, was no match for the Zero. P-39 losses in the defence of Port Moresby were substantial. Heat, humidity, poor maintenance and disease took their toll of the Airacobra pilots. (*Philip Jarrett*)

A5Ms until May 1942, when she received 16 Zeros prior to the Aleutians action.

On 4 June, one of these aircraft, piloted by PO 1st Class Tadayoshi Koga, was hit by anti-aircraft fire and came down on the almost uninhabited island of Akutan. Koga attempted an emergency landing, but the aircraft turned over and he was killed. The Zero and its luckless pilot were found by an American patrol five weeks later. The A6M2 Model 21 was repairable, and was shipped to the Assembly and Repair Department at Naval Air Station North Island, San Diego. It was the first Zero to fall into American hands more or less intact, and, as we shall see later, it was restored to flying condition and extensively evaluated.

On 24 August 1942, during the Battle of the Eastern Solomons, strike aircraft from the *Ryujo* were intercepted by Grumman Wildcats from Guadalcanal and heavily defeated; the *Ryujo* herself was sunk in an attack by 30 SBD dive-bombers and eight Avengers. Some of her aircraft managed to land on Rabaul, but all her fighters were lost when they had to ditch. Most of the pilots were picked up.

The action that became known as the Battle of Santa Cruz was the climax of a Japanese plan to neutralize and capture Guadalcanal's vital airstrip, Henderson Field, as a preliminary to the destruction of the remaining US forces in the Solomons. At this point the US Navy had only two carriers in the area, the USS *Enterprise* and USS *Hornet*, the latter having replaced the USS *Saratoga*, damaged by a submarine torpedo on 31 August and withdrawn to Pearl Harbor for repair. The Americans had also lost the light carrier USS *Wasp*, sunk by a submarine on 15 September while escorting a troop convoy to Guadalcanal.

Battle of Santa Cruz

To activate their plan, the Japanese naval forces put to sea from Truk on 11 October. They included the Carrier Striking Force with the *Shokaku* and *Zuikaku*, the light carrier *Zuiho* – now fully fitted out – and seven destroyers; the Advance Striking Force with two new carriers, the *Junyo* and *Hiyo*, supported by two battleships, five cruisers and 13 destroyers; and the Battleship Striking Force, with two battleships, three cruisers and eight destroyers.

On 26 October the carrier task forces made contact almost simultaneously and launched their strike aircraft. The Japanese force, in two

The Hawker Hurricane, seen here at an airstrip in northern Burma, came face-to-face with the Zero in the battle for the Dutch East Indies and again during the attack on Ceylon in April 1942. In Burma, the Hurricane's main adversary was the Nakajima Ki.43 *Hayabusa* fighter, known as the 'Oscar'. (*Robert Jackson*)

waves 45 minutes apart, comprised 42 Aichi D3A2 dive-bombers, 36 Mitsubishi B5N2 'Kate' torpedo-bombers, and 55 Zero fighters from the *Shokaku*, *Zuikaku* and *Zuiho*; the USS *Hornet* and *Enterprise* launched three waves comprising 20 SBD Dauntlesses, 20 TBM Avengers and 24 F4F Wildcats. While these forces were en route, two SBDs from the *Enterprise*, on an armed reconnaissance, encountered the *Zuiho* and bombed her, damaging her flight deck and rendering it unusable.

At 09.40, purely by chance, the opposing air groups ran into each other and a brief air battle developed in which the Zeros shot down three SBDs and four Wildcats for the loss of five of their own. At 10.10, the first Japanese wave located the *Hornet* and subjected her to a bomb and torpedo attack that left her burning and listing in the water.

Thirty minutes later, the *Hornet*'s strike aircraft also found the *Shokaku* and scored four hits with 450-kg (1000-lb) bombs, putting the carrier out of the battle. She limped back to Japan to undergo repairs, a process that would last until the end of February 1943.

The Japanese second wave attacked the *Enterprise*, scoring three bomb hits; torpedo

attacks were frustrated by Wildcat combat air patrols. Further attacks in the afternoon, launched by the *Zuikaku* and *Junyo*, succeeded in sinking the crippled *Hornet*. Fortunately for the Americans, the Japanese were unable to exploit their tactical success. They had exhausted their fuel reserves and were compelled to withdraw to Truk to replenish.

Equal terms

The air fighting in the Solomons clearly showed that the Zero, while still superior to the American types it encountered, no longer enjoyed the complete mastery of the air that had been the hallmark of its operations in the early months of the Pacific war.

During this period it was the Grumman F4F Wildcat that held the line, and as the US Navy and Marine Corps pilots gained more combat experience and developed better tactics, they began to take an increasing toll of the enemy. And, in terms of equipment, much better prospects were just over the horizon.

Taking note of the lessons learned in action by the Wildcat squadrons, the Grumman Aircraft Company designed a larger and more powerful fighter, the F6F Hellcat, which entered

Grumman F6F Hellcats of Navy Fighter Squadron VF-8, pictured in 1943. The beefy Hellcat was the first American fighter to meet the Zero on equal terms. Numerical superiority, and better training and tactics, combined to give it a distinct advantage in the crucial year of 1944. (*Philip Jarrett*)

service in 1943 and which at last gave the US Navy pilots a chance to meet the Zeros on more or less equal terms.

Before the war ended, the Hellcat squadrons would be officially credited with the destruction of nearly 5000 enemy aircraft, or 80 per cent of all the kills registered by American carrier pilots during World War II.

Another new American type that made its appearance in the Pacific theatre in 1943 was the twin-engined, twin-tailed Lockheed P-38 Lightning. Already in service in Europe, the long-range Lightning substantially increased the radius that could be covered by land-based American fighter squadrons.

One of the most famous of all operations carried out by the Lightning took place on 18 April 1943, when P-38s of the 339th Fighter Squadron, USAAF, shot down a G4M bomber carrying Admiral Isoroku Yamamoto, the Japanese Navy Commander-in-Chief. To do the job, the P-38s made an 1770-km (1100-mile) round trip from Guadalcanal to intercept Yamamoto's aircraft over Kahili Atoll.

The bomber (together with a second, carrying Yamamoto's staff) was escorted by six Zeros of Air Group 204 from Rabaul, led by Lt (Jg) Takeshi. One reason for the comparatively light escort was that the Japanese command at Rabaul did not believe that any US aircraft could present a threat at such a range; the Japanese were also unaware that the Americans had deciphered their Navy code, so that the exact timing of Yamamoto's flight was known.

Gull-winged Corsair

Early in 1943 some US Navy and Marine squadrons began to rearm with a powerful new fighter, the Chance Vought F4U Corsair. One pilot in particular achieved spectacular successes while flying this type; he was Lt Bob Hanson, a member of Marine Squadron VMF-215, and he rose to fame in the embattled sky over Rabaul. On 14 January 1944 Hanson

The twin-engined, twin-tail Lockheed P-38 Lightning was widely used in the Pacific from 1943. Much faster than the Zero, it leaped into the headlines when aircraft of the USAAF's 339th Fighter Squadron shot down the G4M bomber that was carrying Admiral Yamamoto on a tour of inspection. (*Philip Jarrett*)

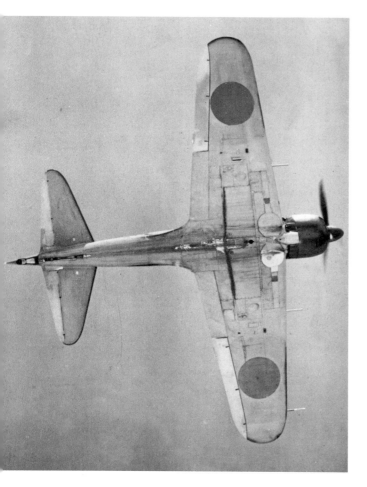

The Zero was a neat, workmanlike, no-frills design, as this photograph of the aircraft's underside shows. Later in its career, the Zero's performance suffered as equipment changes made the aircraft progressively heavier, with no appreciable power increase to compensate for the extra weight. (*Philip Jarrett*)

rapidly assumed a superiority that would never be lost. They often gained formidable successes in dogfights that were often unbelievably one-sided. In April 1943, for example, four P-38 Lightnings were carrying out a sweep over Guadalcanal at 9455 m (31,000 ft) when they sighted three Zeros lower down. The P-38s dived to the attack and shot all three Zeros down in quick succession.

Climbing again, the American pilots sighted a formation of Zeros attacking some Wildcats at 8540 m (28,000 feet). The Lightnings burst through the middle of the fight at high speed in a shallow dive, knocking down two Zeros as they went. The Japanese broke in all directions and took evasive action, but two more Zeros went down in flames. In less than 20 minutes the four P-38s had accounted for seven of the enemy with no loss or damage to themselves.

Hellcat dominant

But in 1944, it was the Grumman Hellcat that ruled the Pacific sky, its superiority culminating in the massive air battle that was to go down in history as the 'Great Marianas Turkey Shoot'. It happened in June 1944, during the Battle of the Philippine Sea, when waves of Japanese aircraft attacked the US task force that was undertaking a major amphibious operation to occupy key objectives in the Marianas.

On the 19th, with the amphibious invasion in full swing, large numbers of Japanese bombers and torpedo-bombers made a series of desperate attempts to hit the task force; they were detected by radar at a range of 240 km (150 miles), and the carrier fighters were waiting for them. The powerful Hellcats swarmed all over the attackers before they even sighted the carriers, and of the 200 Japanese aircraft in the first two strike waves, only 30 escaped. At the close of the day, the Japanese had lost a staggering 402 aircraft.

End of the carriers

The Battle of the Philippine Sea saw the end of the carrier *Shokaku*, sunk on 19 June 1944, and the large new armoured-deck carrier *Taiho*, sunk on the same day, both by American submarines. Earlier, these two carriers, together with the *Zuikaku*, had launched 96 aircraft of Air Group 601, including 32 Zeros, at the US

fought the first of a series of combats that would set a record, destroying five out of a formation of 70 Zeros that were trying to intercept American bombers. His next five sorties over Rabaul netted him one Zero, three Zeros, four Zeros, three Zeros and four Zeros, which brought his score to over 20 enemy aircraft destroyed in a period of only 17 days.

As new American fighter types arrived in the Pacific, the Japanese began to suffer combat losses that were little short of staggering, and the US pilots, now skilfully led by veterans with two years' of experience behind them,

Zero fighters preparing for a mission. A principal factor in the Zero's early success was its excellent combat radius. This was extended further by the use of long-range auxiliary fuel tanks, seen in this photograph, and the use of highly economical cruising speeds, the result of much pre-war experimentation. (*Philip Jarrett*)

Task Force 58; 75 per cent of them were destroyed. Air Group 601 had been organised around the the former 1st Carrier Division Air Group in February 1944, for service aboard *Shokaku*, *Zuikaku* and *Taiho*; its original complement had included 81 Zero fighters.

Zuikaku survived for a few more months, until she was sunk off Cape Engano during the Battle of Leyte Gulf on 25 October 1944. Three more carriers, *Zuiho*, *Chitose* and *Chiyoda*, were also lost on that day, marking the effective end of Japanese naval air power.

During the Battle of Leyte Gulf, however, the Japanese launched a new and terrifying weapon at the American task forces: the *kamikaze* (Divine Wind) suicide aircraft. On 25 October, five Zero pilots of the newly formed Special Attack Corps, led by Lt Yorio Seki, attacked five US escort carriers, sinking one and badly damaging four others.

Kamikaze

Altogether, 331 Zeros were launched at Allied shipping during the struggle for the Philippines between October 1944 and January 1945. Of

these, 158 reached the target area, and although not all managed to dive into a ship, those that did exacted a terrible toll. It was a pattern that was to be repeated during the early months of 1945, culminating in the Battle of Okinawa. During the critical period of this battle (6 April to 28 May), the Japanese expended some 1500 aircraft in suicide attacks on Task Force 58, aiming principally at the vital carriers. Although none was lost, 15 were hit, eight of them heavy units, together with numerous smaller vessels.

More Zeros were used in these attacks than any other type. The survivors, starved of fuel, fought on in the defence of the Japanese homeland, now under attack by carrier aircraft as well as B-29 bombers. In August 1945, Japanese *kamikaze* units prepared to sacrifice themselves in a massive last-ditch suicide mission against the expected Allied invasion fleet. But the detonation of atomic bombs over Hiroshima and Nagasaki brought the war to an end and that final operation of the Pacific war, with all the massive loss of life it would have entailed, was never carried out.

The A6M2 Model 21 Zero that came down on Akutan island in the Aleutians, killing its pilot, was assessed as repairable and was shipped to a naval repair depot to be restored to flying condition. These photographs show it in American markings, being evaluated by US pilots. (*Philip Jarrett*)

3. Zero People:
Engineers and Aces

Jiro Horikoshi, the principal designer of the Zero, wrote the definitive history of its development.

'Japanese naval aviation was chiefly British in its ancestry, while the Army drew heavily from French and German sources. These were the easy old days, after I received my degree in aeronautics from the Imperial University in Tokyo and entered the Nagoya Aircraft Works of Mitsubishi Heavy Industries Ltd as a design calculator – or subordinate structures engineer. This was the period during which Japanese industry was trying to catch up with the more advanced technical status of certain Western powers by hiring experts and buying ideas and experience.

'By the time I entered Mitsubishi, at the age of 23, the noted British designer, Mr Smith, and his party were no longer with the company. The noted French designer, M. Vernisse, was employed in the concern, as was Mr Petty from Blackburn Aircraft Co. in England, and his assistants, Mr Bolton and Mr Wilkinson. These men stayed for contracts ranging from one to three years during the formative period between 1926 and 1931. They designed aircraft, taught other engineers the techniques of design. Unfortunately, I was in the lower ecehelon. My task was supervising stress calculations, and I had no opportunity to contact these foreign experts directly.

'The importation of foreign experts was universally practised during this period when Japan's infant aircraft industry was gathering momentum. Nakajima, Kawasaki, Aichi, Tachikawa – all of these had experts from abroad on their payrolls. Their influence during this period can be seen directly in the aeroplanes that were acquired by the Army and Navy. During this period, Japanese companies went heavily into the purchase of patent licences of all kinds. For example, the Handley Page-Lachman leading edge wing slot was acquired jointly by Mitsubishi and Tachikawa for ¥100,000. Licences for accessories, engines instruments and the like were purchased wholesale, to permit the infant industry to get into a competitive position.

'I was sent abroad to study during this period, and from June to December, 1929, I travelled in Europe – England, France, Germany and the Netherlands, visiting aeroplane factories. I stayed with the Junkers company for three months, studying their procedure in design. In December, 1929, I embarked for the United States, where I visited many plants. I stayed several months at the Curtiss Company's plant in Garden City, where I acted as inspector for the P-6 pursuit aircraft that had been purchased by Mitsubishi.

Home-grown ideas

'When I got home in the early autumn of 1930, there was a new movement in the air. Japanese designers had a feeling that they wanted to try their own ideas in designing. By 1932, the Japanese Government was about ready to listen. The Japanese Navy was particularly anxious to start a new line of aircraft, built entirely by Japanese. They ordered three

This photograph illustrates the Zero's exceptionally clean aerodynamic lines. The fighter would have been still cleaner had it been fitted with an in-line engine, but radials were lighter – and in any case no suitable in-line powerplants of sufficient power were available in Japan at the time of the Zero's inception. (*Philip Jarrett*)

important types under this programme, a carrier fighter, a carrier torpedo-bomber and a reconnaissance seaplane. Nakajima and Mitsubishi got orders for the carrier jobs, and I was appointed chief designer of the carrier fighter, chiefly on the basis of my experience and knowledge of fighters gained by contact with the P-6. None of the machines presented for the *7-Shi* competition met the Navy's requirements. Nakajima had presented a carrier version of the old Army Type 91 fighter, evolved by the French designer Marie.

'Ours didn't fare too well. The original prototype shed a stabiliser during a power dive test. Luckily, the pilot baled out without any trouble. The second prototype went into a flat spin during an aerobatic test, and went into the deck from a double roll. The pilot, Lt Okamura, got out all right.

'By 1934 the Navy eased up on size and range demands for their carrier fighters and dive-bombers. By this time I had a lot more experience and a few more original ideas. When the call came for the *9-Shi* fighter, I conceived long, slim lines for the new ship instead of thick, stubby ones.

Dogfighting idea

'Most of the leading Navy pilots had the greater part of their experience on the old biplane fighters. They conceded the need for speed and climb, but their tactical concept ideas

still called for a tight turning circle, the old dogfighting idea. To get the combination of speed and manoeuvrability into the aeroplane I desired, the only answer was a light aeroplane.

Fixed gear

'We retained the fixed landing gear in the design, since the gear consituted only 10 per cent of the overall drag. A retractable gear would have raised the top speed from 399 km/h (248 mph) to 410–415 km/h (255–258 mph). We did not figure that the increased weight and mechanical complexity of the retraction mechanism was worth the investment.

'The *9-Shi* incorporated the use of tension-field spar webs, an idea that was brought to Japan by Capt. Wada, who later became Vice-Admiral and Chief of the Navy's Air Headquarters. This system permitted considerable reduction of the wing structure weight, without sacrificing strength. The *9-Shi* was the first aeroplane in Japan to use flush riveting, and was probably the second design in the world to do so. The first, I believe, was the Heinkel He 70.

'The first *9-Shi* prototype was test flown at Kagamigahara Field in February, 1935. It had a top speed of 450 km/h (280 mph), 100 km/h (63 mph) faster than the old *7-Shi* and the Type 95 carrier fighter that it was built to replace. The fabric-covered Nakajima machines, built

A formation of A6M3 Model 22 fighters of the 251st Air Group in flight over the Solomons. This group normally carried the unit code U1 on the fin; it appears to have been overpainted when a dark green camouflage pattern was applied over the original sky grey finish. (*Philip Jarrett*)

unsuccessfully for the competition, were sold to the newspaper *Asahi* for liaison work.

'The first *9-Shi* was an inverted gull-wing type, built without flaps. The ship developed a pitching motion at high angles of attack, due to the turbulent flow at the V-shaped concave part on the upper surface of the wing. Thus, despite the better visibility and the weight saving afforded by this configuration, the second *9-Shi* had a straight centre section.

High performance

'The *9-Shi* was undoubtedly, as the Americans would say, a 'hot ship'. A shallow approach was required, and the ship had a decided ballooning tendency on touch-down. It was thoroughly tested under the supervision of Lt-Cdr Yoshito Kobayashi, chief test pilot of the flight test section. Its virtues were noted, particularly its speed. Its faults were analysed, and corrective measures taken. Then the ship was used for static testing.

'The second *9-Shi* was fitted with a split flap and a larger engine, a direct-drive type, since the first machine had developed some trouble with the reduction gear system. This machine suited the rigid requirements of the Navy. On the basis of its performance, the Navy tried to cancel an order for French Dewoitine D.510s. They finally had to take two, which were kept, chiefly for the study of the engine-mounted cannon. The noted French pilot Marcel Doret flew the planes on demonstration for us. We flew comparative tests against the *9-Shi* at Kasumigaura Navy Field, and the Mitsubishi machine proved superior on almost every point of performance.

'The gap between the final approval of the *9-Shi* airframe and its adoption as a military machine stemmed from our inability to produce a suitable powerplant. A number of radial engines, varying from 600 to 800 hp, were considered by the Navy. Finally, the smallest unit, the Nakajima Kotobuki 2-1, was adopted because it was the most reliable unit in production. The *9-Shi* machine went into service with the designation of Type 96-1 Carrier Fighter (A5M1).

'During the time when the 96 was the leading Japanese fighter, we had the opportunity of running comparative tests against the American Seversky P-35. We purchased ten of these for purposes of test and study, and found that the machines were heavy, unmanoeuvrable, and did not compare with the performance of the Type 96 in virtually all major points. Actual combat against the Gloster Gladiator, the Curtiss Hawk 75 and the Russian I-15 and I-16 indicated that for most purposes we had the superior machine. However, the Navy was not deluded into believing that these tests made us the tops in fighter design; it stood to reason that no country was going to export its best aircraft. For that reason, we were encouraged to improve our design and keep step with the world.

Speed and climb

'The Navy determined that the next machine, which was to be faster and have reasonably proportionate performance, must retain greater manoeuvrability than opposing aircraft. In fact, the Navy air strategists wanted speed and climb, but they still demanded a tight turning circle. These were exacting demands; the sole solution appeared to be in building the lightest possible airframe and keeping the wing loading as low as possible. Navy requirements did not contain consideration of such things as fire protection, self-sealing tanks, armour plate, and anything else that was weight consuming.

'We knew that Japan had limited resources. Therefore, it was important that the aeroplanes that we did produce were superior to those they might meet in combat. I had laid down three criteria for the design of a fighter: performance, producibility, and ease of maintenance. For a small country, performance was the major object – even at the cost of the other two, or even the safety of the crews.

'It was against this background of virtually impossible demands that we began work on the *12-Shi* prototype in 1937.'

Impossible demands or not, Jiro Horikoshi and his engineering team rose to meet them admirably, and produced an aircraft that was a fighter pilot's delight. The official definition of an 'ace' is a pilot who has destroyed at least five enemy aircraft in air combat. The Japanese record starts at eight victories, and 149 Imperial Navy Zero pilots (some of whom flew other types in the closing months of the war) destroyed eight or more to achieve 'ace' status. Dozens of others must have shot down five or more, but their names are unrecorded.

Of the 149 mentioned above, 59 survived the war, a surprisingly high number, given the Japanese penchant for self-destruction, and one that compares quite favourably with the *Luftwaffe*'s ratio, although some of the Japanese pilots are known to have been withdrawn from combat because of wounds or other disabilities.

There is no reason to doubt the claims made by the Japanese aces. The official Japanese bulletins, on the other hand, became increasingly outrageous in their claims of Allied aircraft destroyed as the war went on. During air attacks on Rabaul on 2 November 1943, for example, the Japanese records state that 119 Allied aircraft were shot down; the true figure was 19. Similarly, the Japanese admitted to a loss of 18 fighters; the Allies claimed 68. And over a two-day period, 16 to 17 February 1945, the Japanese claimed to have destroyed 98 Allied carrier aircraft in attacks on the homeland for the loss of 30 of their own. Allied figures claimed 332 enemy aircraft destroyed in combat, 177 on the ground, at a cost of 47 Allied aircraft which did not return.

Leading ace

As far as it is possible to establish, the leading Japanese ace of the Pacific war was Lt (Jg) Hiroyoshi Nishizawa, who completed his flying training in March 1939 and was assigned to the Chitose Air Group in 1941. In February 1942 he was transferred to the 4th Air Group and moved to Rabaul, scoring his first victory on the 3rd. In April he was transferred to the Tainan Air Group, which deployed to Lae, New Guinea. On 7 August, the day that saw the American assault on Guadalcanal, he shot down six F4F Wildcats in a single air battle, though he only just made it back to his base with a damaged aircraft. By November 1942, when the Tainan Air Group was redesignated Air Group 251, his score had risen to 30.

The A6M5 Zero appeared in prototype form in August 1943, and was in full production by March the following year. The A6M5b Model 52 was probably the best version of the Zero to see combat, and could hold its own against the more powerful but slightly less manoeuvrable Grumman F6F Hellcat. (*Philip Jarrett*)

After a spell in Japan Nishizawa rejoined Air Group 251 and moved with it to Rabaul in May 1943. It is recorded that he destroyed six aircraft in mid-June, but his subsequent achievements are not clear because the air groups discontinued the practice of recording the scores of individual pilots around this time. In September 1943 he was transferred to Air Group 253 for a brief period before returning to Japan, where in November he was promoted to Warrant Officer and assigned to Air Group 203, which was engaged in air defence duties in the northern Kuriles.

In October 1944 the units moved to the Philippines, and on the 25th Nishizawa led a flight of three Zeros that flew in direct support of the first planned *kamikaze* attack of the war. He shot down two Hellcats during this operation, but had to make an emergency landing on the island of Cebu, short of fuel. The next day, he was returning to base in a transport, having been compelled to leave his own aircraft behind, when it was attacked and shot down by two Hellcats over Calapan, Mindoro island. Nishizawa was killed, along with everyone else on board. He was posthumously promoted to Lt (Jg), a not uncommon practice in the Japanese Navy.

For reasons explained earlier, Nishizawa's final score has been difficult to determine accurately. Some sources put it as high as 150, which is unlikely; for a long time, the 'official' tally was fixed at 102, although this has since been revised to 87 in the light of more recent documentary evidence.

Top scorer?

Because of the uncertainty surrounding Nishizawa's victories, it is possible that another Zero pilot, Lt (Jg) Tetsuzo Iwamoto, may have beaten him to first place. Iwamoto first saw combat with the 12th Air Group in China on 25 February 1938, flying an A5M, when he shot down five enemy aircraft during the attack on Nanchang. By September, when he returned to Japan, he had flown 82 sorties and destroyed 14 aircraft, becoming the leading ace of the Sino-Japanese conflict. In the Pacific war, he served on board the carrier *Zuikaku* and took part in the operations at Pearl Harbor, Ceylon, and in the Coral Sea before being transferred as an instructor in August 1942. In 1943 he served successively with Air Group 281 on northern area air defence, and then with Air Groups 204 and 253 at Rabaul and Truk.

In June 1944 Iwamoto returned to Japan, serving on air defence duties. Promoted to Ensign, he saw further action in the Philippines and Taiwan before returning once more to Japan, where he fought on with Air Group 203, taking part in the great air battles over Okinawa and the homeland. Iwamoto survived the war, only to die from natural causes shortly afterwards. He himself always claimed that he had destroyed 202 aircraft, 142 of them as the result of battles in the Rabaul area. A realistic appraisal puts his score somewhere in the 80s, which makes it entirely possible that he might have been Japan's leading ace ahead of Nishizawa.

Yamamoto's escort

Japan's third-ranking ace, Ensign Sho-ichi Sugita, was unfortunate in that he was one of the Zero pilots who failed to protect Admiral Yamamoto during the admiral's fateful flight in April 1943. Graduating from flight school in March 1942, Sugita was assigned to Air Group 204 and for a year was operational in the Solomons area, based at Buin. His first kill, a B-17, came over Buin on 1 December 1942.

On 18 April, 1943, he was one of six Zero pilots escorting Admiral Yamamoto's G4M bomber on an inspection tour when it was attacked by P-38s and destroyed. It was Sugita who shot down the only P-38 to be lost on this mission, that flown by Lt Ray Hine. On 26 August 1943 his aircraft was hit and set on fire; he parachuted to safety, but suffered burns over most of his body. He returned to action in March 1944, operating in the Marianas and Caroline Islands with Air Group 263, and was in combat over the Philippines later in the year.

In January 1945 he was posted to the newly formed Air Group 343, flying the Kawanishi N1K *Shiden* (Allied code-name 'George') in the battle for Okinawa and in the defence of Japan. On 15 April 1945, while taking off from Kanoya to intercept an incoming raid, the airfield was attacked by Allied fighters and Sugita died in the blazing wreckage of his aircraft. Sugita was credited with the destruction of 70 aircraft.

Best-known ace

Probably the best-known Japanese air ace was Lt (Jg) Saburo Sakai, mainly because he wrote *Samurai!*, a book about his exploits, which was translated into several languages. Sakai graduated top of his class at flight school, and in September 1938 he was posted to the 12th Air Group for operations in central China, claiming his first combat victory on 5 October near Hankow. In June 1941 he was promoted to Petty Officer 1st Class, and in October he was transferred to the Tainan Air Group. As a flight commander, he took part in the air battles during the Philippines and Dutch East Indies campaigns, afterwards operating from Rabaul and Lae, New Guinea.

Early in the battle for Guadalcanal Sakai was hit by return fire from the gunner of a TBD Avenger and received severe head wounds, but despite his injuries he managed to return to Rabaul and was shipped back to Japan. According to official records, his score at this point was 28. He returned to operations later in the war, but failing eyesight compelled him to give up combat flying, and he ended the war as

Captured Zero pictured after the end of the war. Note the bullet holes on the hangar wall, the result of strafing attacks by Allied fighters. Many Japanese fighter pilots could have fought on, had it not been for the fact that fuel reserves were practically non-existent. (*Philip Jarrett*)

Saburo Sakai (standing extreme left) poses with other Zero pilots of the Tainan Air Group at Lae, on the northern coast of New Guinea. In spite of operating under extremely primitive conditions, the Lae unit was a constant thorn in the side af Allied units fighting to force the Japanese off the huge island. (via *Chris Bishop*)

a fighter instructor, with an official score of 64 aircraft destroyed. An account of one of Saburo Sakai's last air battles, on 4 July, 1944, gives a clear idea of the odds the Japanese fighter pilots were facing at this period of the Pacific War.

Impossible odds

'The formation of Japanese Navy aircraft droned steadily on over the featureless waters of the Pacific. There were seventeen of them: eight twin-engined Mitsubishi G4M "Betty" bombers escorted by nine A6M Zero fighters. An hour earlier, the aircraft had taken off in a cloud of volcanic dust from the bomb-shattered airstrip on the island of Iwo Jima. For two days, American carrier aircraft had struck at the island in overwhelming force, destroying

installations and virtually wiping out the Japanese combat squadrons based there. At the end of those two days, the Imperial Japanese Navy's original complement of 80 Zero fighters on the island had been reduced to nine, while the eight "Betty" bombers were all that remained of an original wing of 50 machines.

'What was left of the Japanese Naval Air Arm on Iwo was being pitted against impossible odds. Somewhere ahead of the formation, detected by a reconnaissance aircraft the previous day, lay a large American task force, and Japanese Intelligence guessed that its destination was Iwo Jima. Intelligence, in fact, was only partly correct; although part of the task force had been detailed to bombard Iwo, the bulk of it was destined for the Philippines.

Captured A6M5 Zero of Air Group 261, as indicated by the unit code on the tail. Nicknamed the *Tora* or 'Tiger' unit, Air Group 261 was established on 1 June 1943 at Kagoshima. The group was disbanded on 10 July 1944, after losing all its aircraft in the battle for Saipan. (*Philip Jarrett*)

The view of the Zero most dreaded by Allied aircrew. Even when it was past its best, the Zero could still be a deadly weapon in the hands of an ace such as Hiroyoshi Nishizawa. Nishizawa was an unlikely ace: before enlisting in the Imperial Japanese Navy, he had worked in a textile factory. (*Philip Jarrett*)

'Japanese Naval Air Command had ordered every available aircraft on Iwo Jima to launch an immediate attack on the enemy. When the order first came through there had been plenty of machines to do the job; but then the US carrier aircraft had launched three massive strikes on the island. In the last raid alone, 40 Zeros had been destroyed, either in the air or on the ground. The survivors were now on their way to carry out their hopeless mission. The Zeros flew in three "vics", shepherding the lumbering bombers. The crews of fighters and

bombers alike knew that in a very short time they were likely to die. Once in the target area they were each to select an enemy ship and dive into it.

'Leading the third "vic" of Zeros, Ensign Saburo Sakai was filled with a deep sense of futility. Before sacrificing their own lives, the Zero pilots had the task of ensuring that the bombers broke through the enemy defences – and the carriers of the US task force could put up 400 fighters. Nine against 400 was long odds, even for experienced pilots like Sakai,

The pilot of an A6M2 Model 21 Zero runs up his engine prior to take-off. Most Model 21 Zeros were initially finished in light grey overall, with a black engine cowling and silver spinner. Dark green camouflage was adopted late in 1942. (*via J.R. Cavanagh*)

whose combat career had begun in China in the late 1930s.

'The formation passed the black, bare rock that was Pagan Island, the first sight of land since leaving Iwo. Forty minutes later, a line of towering storm clouds rose above the horizon; somewhere beneath them lay the American warships. The Japanese began a gradual descent from 16,000 to 13,000 feet. The pilots would begin their death-dive as soon as the warships were sighted, building up speed in the faint hope of evading the fighters that were sure to be waiting, alerted by radar.

'A minute later, the glitter of sunlight on a wing surface ahead and above caught Sakai's eye. More flashes, and an avalanche of American fighters came tumbling down towards the Japanese. They were F6F Hellcats, and there were at least twenty of them. In line astern they ripped through the Japanese formation, firing as they went. The two leading "Bettys" disintegrated in a cloud of flame and

debris as the torpedoes they carried exploded. Two more Hellcat formations, more than fifty fighters, converged on the Japanese. The Zero pilots had orders to avoid combat, but this was now impossible ... A Hellcat flashed through Sakai's sights and he fired; the enemy fighter went into a series of uncontrollable flick rolls and plunged down, trailing smoke.

'The Zero pilots were soon fighting isolated battles for their lives as the "Bettys" were hacked out of the sky. In under a minute seven of the bombers were destroyed, their charred remains fluttering down towards the ocean beneath spreading clouds of black smoke. Two Zeros went down, balls of brilliant flame.

Swirling darkness

'Sakai realized that it was pointless to fight on; the odds were too overwhelming. Gradually, in the middle of a whirling mass of Hellcats, his two wingmen sticking to him like glue, he edged his way towards a large storm cloud.

A6M3 Zero of the Oita Air Group. This was one of the groups responsible for air combat training, and many Japanese air aces were assigned to it as instructors during recuperation from wounds or in their brief rests from front-line combat duty. (*via J.R. Cavanagh*)

Lt-Cdr Kiyokuma Heajima of the 863rd Flying Group (*Kokutai*) accompanied by his wing man sits in front of his A6M5 Zero 52. Entering service late in 1943, the A6M5 was the most numerous Japanese Navy fighter in the last years of the war, with more than 1,700 examples being built. (*via Chris Bishop*)

The pilot of an A6M2 Zero takes a last look around before take-off. Some units operating in the Pacific islands had the white disk surrounding the rising sun (*Hinomaru*) insignia deleted for reasons of camouflage. The *Hinomaru* itself was also toned down to a duller red. (*via J.R. Cavanagh*)

Seizing their chance, the three Zeros dived between two groups of Hellcats and plunged into the sheltering cloud. For endless minutes they fell through swirling darkness, their machines buffeted by severe turbulence in the heart of the cumulus, eventually dropping from the cloud base a few hundred feet over a sea lashed by torrential rain.

Mission abandoned

'The three fighters re-formed and turned south, still searching for the American ships. The pilots saw nothing but the blinding rain, lashing the sea into a fury and reducing visibility to only a few hundred yards. They flew on for another half hour, with the visibility growing worse all the time and dusk beginning to creep over the sea. In the end Sakai realized the hopelessness of their task; fighting an inner battle against his long years of strict discipline and training, requiring him to obey orders without question, he decided to abandon the mission. The three Zeros turned and set course for Iwo Jima.

'Three hours later, they landed in darkness on the island's airstrip. One other Zero pilot had also found his way back, together with the sole surviving "Betty" bomber. The latter's pilot had found the ships, released his torpedo and run for it, evading the prowling Hellcats by a miracle. He, too, had broken the strict ties of discipline and refused to throw away his life needlessly. The following day, sixteen American warships appeared off Iwo Jima. They were unopposed. Their first salvo blasted the airstrip and wiped out the four Zeros that had fought their way back only a few hours earlier. How different it had been only two years ago, when the Zero was mistress of the Pacific skies!'

(Extract from *Fighter Aces of World War II*, by Robert Jackson, Arthur Barker 1976/Corgi 1978)

The pilot of the fourth Zero that made it back to Iwo Jima was Lt (Jg) Kaneyoshi Muto, a talented pilot who went on to achieve a tally of around 28 victories – the actual figure is uncertain. Muto gained the first of his kills over China, and was posted to the 3rd Air Group in September 1941. Flying as wingman to Lt

An A6M5 Zero shows its underside. The join just aft of the wing trailing edge, where the two fuselage halves are bolted together, is clearly visible in this photograph. Although Allied fighters later outstripped the Zero in terms of speed, they never matched it in manoeuvrability. (*Philip Jarrett*)

An A6M5 Zero found in an aircraft 'graveyard' at the end of the war. In the closing months of the conflict Japanese manufacturers were producing some exciting new combat aircraft, but such was the ferocity of the American strategic bombing campaign that only a trickle reached the squadrons. (*via J.R. Cavanagh*)

Tamotsu Yokoyama, the group commander, he saw a good deal of action over the Philippines and Dutch East Indies. In April 1942 he was transferred to Air Group 252, which advanced to Rabaul in November. He remained with this group until November 1943, after which he was posted to the Yokosuka Air Group for home air defence duties.

In 1945 June 1945, at the special request of Captain Minoru Genda, he was transferred to Air Group 343, equipped with Kawanishi N1K *Shiden-kai* fighters. Muto replaced Ensign Sho-ichi Sugita, killed in action earlier. Muto was himself shot down and killed in an air battle over the Bungo Strait on 24 July 1945, three weeks before Japan's surrender.

Brilliant pilot

One of the most brilliant Japanese fighter pilots, and one who would almost certainly have gone on to notch up a score to rival those of Nishizawa and Sakai, was Warrant Officer Toshio Ota. Like Nishizawa and Sakai, Ota was assigned to the Tainan Air Group, and gained his first combat victory over Luzon on 8 December 1941. On 29 January 1942 he was wounded in a running battle with a B-17 over Balikpapan, Borneo. Returning to action in April, he moved with the group to Rabaul, experiencing many air combats before participating in the battle for Guadalcanal in August. On 21 October, 1942, Ota failed to return from an operational sortie. At that time, he was officially credited with 34 enemy aircraft destroyed.

Close behind Ota, with an official score of 32, came Warrant Officer Kazuo Sugino. His first combat did not take place until 2 November 1943, when he shot down three enemy aircraft. From then until March 1944, when he returned to Japan to serve as an instructor, he was in action almost daily. In August 1944 he was transferred to Air Group 634, participating in air battles off Taiwan and over the Philippines.

In February 1945 he was withdrawn from combat and sent to to Taiwan, where he became an instructor with the Hakata Air Group, a formation responsible for training *kamikaze* pilots. He was still there when the war ended. During his career, Sugino amassed a total flight time of 1994 hours and flew 495 operational sorties, about 100 of which involved air combat. He served in the Japanese Maritime Self-Defence Forces after the war.

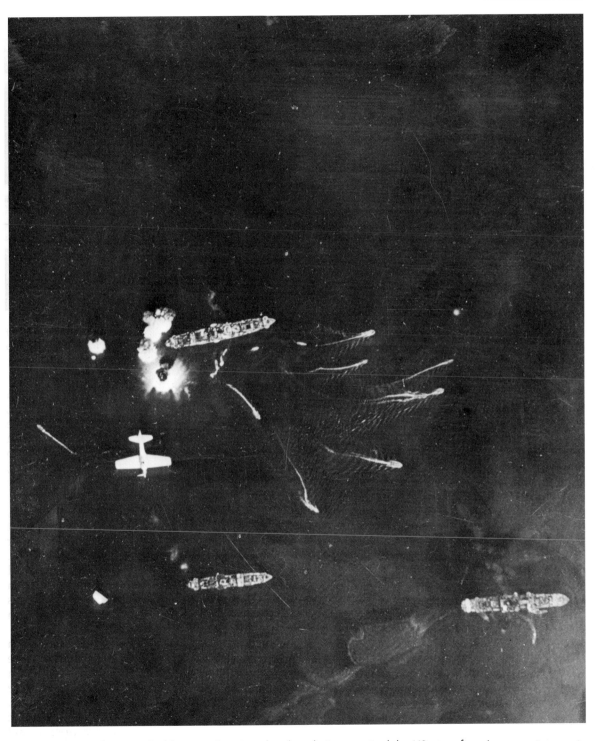

An A6M3 Zero photographed from an American bomber during an attack by US aircraft on Japanese transports in the Solomons, 1943. A bomb explosion has just occurred near the ship at the top. Note the A6M3's distinctive square-cut wingtips. (*Philip Jarrett*)

The business end of the Zero, showing the three-blade propeller. The prototype Zero was fitted with a two-blade variable-pitch propeller, but vibration problems meant that subsequent aircraft used the three-blade Hamilton design built under licence in Japan by Sumitomo. (*via J.R. Cavanagh*)

One member of the Tainan Air Group who attracted much publicity was Lt (Jg) Jun-ichi Sasai, the son of engineer Captain Kenji Sasai. He scored his first victory on 3 February 1942, during an air battle over Java, and his tally increased dramatically in the following months.

'Richthofen of Rabaul'

By the end of July 1942 Sasai boasted that he had shot down 54 enemy aircraft, and that he would soon catch up with the score of the famous German air ace of World War I, Baron Manfred von Richthofen. That opportunity, however, was to be denied him.

On 8 August 1942 he led a flight of eight Zeros to Guadalcanal, engaged in an air battle against 15 F4F Wildcats, and failed to return. Officially, he was credited with the destruction of 27 enemy aircraft. Soon after his death, Sasai was posthumously promoted from Lieutenant (Jg) to Lieutenant-Commander.

Japan's top twenty Zero Aces

Name	Rank	Total	Remarks
Hiroyoshi Nishizawa	Lt(Jg)	87	k.26.10.44
Tetsuzo Iwamoto	Lt(Jg)	c.80	
Sho-ichi Sugita	Ens	c.70	k.15.4.45
Saburo Sakai	Lt(Jg)	64	
Takeo Okumura	CPO	54	k.22.9.43
Toshio Ota	WO	34	k.21.10.42
Kazuo Sugino	WO	32	
Shizuo Ishii	CPO	29	k.24.10.43
Kaneyoshi Muto	Lt(Jg)	28	k.24.7.45
Jun-ichi Sasai	Lt-Cdr	27	k.26.8.42
Sada-aki Akamatsu	Lt(Jg)	27	
Naoshi Kanno	Lt	25	k.1.8.45
Nabuo Ogiya	WO	24	k.13.2.4
Shigeo Sugio	Lt(Jg)	20+	
Kazushi Uto	PO3c	19	k.13.9.42
Ki-ichi Nagano	CPO	19	k.6.11.44
Hiroshi Okano	WO	19	
Masayuke Nakase	PO1c	18	k.9.2.42
Akio Matsuba	Lt(Jg)	18	
Sadamu Komachi	WO	18	

4. Zero Accomplishments: Performance Comparisons

Recovering an almost intact A6M in the Aleutians was a major intelligence coup for the Americans. But the task of repairing Petty Officer Tadayoshi Koga's crashed Zero was by no means simple – American engineers had no technical data to consult. Fortunately, major repair work only needed to be done to the nose, canopy and tail unit, and the broken Sumitomo propeller was replaced by a Hamilton Standard, the two being virtually identical. The repair task was completed by October 1942, and the Zero was sent to San Diego so that it could be evaluated against the various types of US fighters in first-line service at the time. After the Zero was pitted against the Grumman F4F Wildcat in simulated combat, the subsequent report concluded that:

'The Zeke (Zero) is superior to the F4F-4 in speed and climb at all altitudes above 1000 feet and is superior in service ceiling and range. Close to sea level, with the Wildcat in neutral blower, the two aircraft are equal in level speed. During dives the two aircraft are also equal with the exception that the Zeke's engine cuts out in pushovers. There is no comparison between the turning circles of the two aircraft due to the relative wing loading and low stalling speed of the Zeke.

'In view of the foregoing, the F4F type in combat with the Zeke is basically dependent on mutual support, internal protection, and pullouts or turns at high speed where minimum radius is limited by structural or physiological effects of acceleration (assuming that the allowable acceleration on the F4F is greater than that of the Zero). However, advantage should be taken, where possible, of the superiority of the F4F Wildcat in pushovers and rolls at high speed, or in any combination of the two.'

Zero against P-38

A Lockheed P-38F Lightning was flown to San Diego to take its turn with the Zero.

'To begin this test, both ships took off in formation on a pre-arranged signal. The Zero left the ground first and was about 300 feet in the air before the P-38F was airborne. The Zero reached 5000 feet about five seconds ahead of the Lightning. From an indicated sped of 200 mph (174 kt) the Lightning accelerated away from the Zero in straight and level flight quite rapidly. The Zero was superior to the P-38 in manoeuvrability at speeds below 300 mph (260 kt). The planes returned to formation and both ships reduced to their best respective climbing speed. Upon signal the climb was started to 10,000 feet. Again the Zero was slightly superior in straight climbs, reaching 10,000 feet about four seconds ahead of the P-38. Comparable accelerations and turns were tried with the same results.

'In the climb from 15,000 feet to 20,000 feet, the P-38 started gaining at about 18,200 feet. At 20,000 feet the P-38 was superior to the Zero in all manoeuvres except slow speed turns. This advantage was maintained by the P-38 at all altitudes above 20,000 feet. One manoeuvre in which the P-38 was superior to the Zero was a

A captured Zero seen at Wright Field during its evaluation programme. Situated near Dayton, Ohio, Wright was a very important test centre during World War II. In January 1948 the location was renamed Wright-Patterson AFB through the merger of Wright Field and Patterson Field. (*Harry Holmes*)

high speed reversal. It was impossible for the Zero to follow the P-38 in this manoeuvre at speeds above 300 mph (260 kt). The test was continued to 25,000 and 30,000 feet. Due to the superior speed and climb of the P-38F at these altitudes, it could outmanoeuvre the Zero by using these two advantages. The Zero was still superior in slow speed turns.'

Zero against Airacobra

Evaluating the Zero against the Bell P-39D-1 Airacobra produced a few surprising results in the P-39's favour at low to medium altitudes, but higher up there was no doubt at all which was the superior aircraft.

'Take-off was accomplished in formation on signal to initiate a climb from sea level to 5000 feet indicated. The P-39D-1 was drawing 3000 rpm and 70 inches manifold pressure on take-off when the engine started to detonate, so manifold pressure was reduced to 52 inches. The Airacobra left the ground first and arrived at 5000 feet indicated. This manifold pressure of 52 inches could be maintained to 4500 feet indicated. At 5000 feet from a cruising speed of 230 mph (200 kt) indicated, the P-39 reached

10,000 feet approximately six seconds before the Zero. At 10,000 feet indicated, from a cruising speed of 221 mph (191 kt) indicated, the Airacobra still accelerated away from the Zero rapidly.

'Climbing from 10,000 to 15,000 feet, both aircraft maintained equal rates of climb to 12,500 feet. Above this altitude the Zero walked away from the P-39. Climbing from 15,000 feet to 20,000 feet indicated, the Zero took immediate advantage and left the Airacobra. The climb from 20,000 feet to 25,000 feet was not completed as the P-39 was running low on fuel. On a straight climb to altitude from take-off under the same conditions as before, the Airacobra maintained the advantage of the climb until reaching 14,800 feet indicated. Above this altitude the P-39 was left behind, reaching 25,000 feet indicated approximately 5 minutes behind the Zero. At 25,000 feet from a cruising speed of 180 mph (156 kt) indicated, the Zero accelerated away from the P-39 for three ship lengths. This lead was maintained by the Zero for one and a half minutes and it took the P-39D-1 another thirty seconds to gain a lead of one ship length.'

These views of a captured A6M3 Model 32 (Zeke 32) well illustrate the model's angular lines. The aircraft is seen under test at Wright Field in June 1944. (*Philip Jarrett*)

The air intake in the upper lip of the engine cowling, and the squared-off wingtips, were distinguishing features of the A6M3 Zero Model 32, known originally by the code-name of 'Hamp'. When they first encountered the type Allied pilots mistakenly believed that it was an entirely new fighter. (*Philip Jarrett*)

In the hands of an experienced pilot the P-39 could prove a tough opponent for the Zero, as Japanese ace Saburo Sakai discovered. Describing an encounter with some over New Guinea in his book *Samurai*, he wrote:

'The Allied pilots, it appeared, had given serious study to the unexcelled man-oeuvrability we enjoyed with the Zero fighter. Today marked their first attempt at new tactics. We saw the enemy planes over Moresby but, unlike their previous manoeuvres they failed to form into a single large formation. Instead, the enemy planes formed in pairs and trios, and were all over the sky as we approached. Their movements were baffling. If we turned to the left, we'd be hit from above and the right. And so on. If they were trying to confuse us, they were achieving their purpose.

'There was only one thing to do: meet them on their own terms. I pulled up to Sasai's plane and signalled him that I would take the nearest pair of enemy fighters. He nodded and as I pulled away I saw him signalling the other four Zeros into two pairs. We split into three separate groups and turned to meet the enemy. We rushed at the two P-39s I had selected and I

fired a burst at 100 yards. The first Airacobra evaded my shells and winged over into a screaming dive. I had no chance to get near him for another burst.

Desperate manoeuvres

'The second plane was already rolling over for a dive when I rolled hard over to the left, turned, and came out on his tail. For a moment I saw the pilot's startled face as he saw me coming in. The P-39 skidded along on its back, then whipped over again to the left in an attempt to dive. He looked good for Yonekawa, who was glued to my tail. I waved my hand in the cockpit and rolled to the right, leaving the P-39 for my wingman.

'Yonekawa went at the Airacobra like a madman, and I clung to his tail at a distance of 200 yards. The P-39 jinked wildly in a left roll to evade Yonekawa's fire, and Yonekawa took advantage of the bank and turn to narrow the distance between the two planes to about fifty yards. For the next few minutes the two fighters tangled like wildcats, rolling, spiralling, looping, always losing altitude, with Yonekawa clinging grimly to the tail of the

Lieutenant Hideyoki Shingo takes off from the deck of the carrier *Shokaku* just before the Battle of Santa Cruz in October 1942. Although the Zero was still superior to US warplanes, improved US Navy tactics had redressed the balance. *Shokaku* was hit by six bombs from the *Hornet*'s air wing in the battle. (*via Chris Bishop*)

enemy plane and almost leaping out of the way whenever the P-39 turned on his Zero.

'It was a mistake on the part of the enemy pilot to break his dive in the first place. He had every chance of getting away, but now with Yonekawa so close to him, the dive would mean an open and clear shot for the Zero. From 13,000 feet the two planes – with me right behind them – dropped to only 3,000 feet. The enemy pilot, however, knew what he was doing. Unable to shake off the Zero after him, he led the fight back to the Moresby air base and thus within range of the anti-aircraft guns.

'It was by no means a one-sided battle, for the P-39 pilot manouevred brilliantly with an airplane which was out-performed by his pursuer. The Airacobra and Zero looked like whirling dervishes, both firing in short bursts,

and neither pilot scoring any major hits. Soon it became obvious that Yonekawa was gaining the upper hand. On every turn he hung a second or two longer on the tail of the P-39, steadily gaining the advantage. The two planes passed over Moresby and continued their running battle over the thick jungle growth.

'Hatori pulled alongside my own fighter and we gained altitude, circling slowly over the two battling planes. Now they were down to treetop level, where Yonekawa could use the Zero to its best advantage. The Airacobra no longer had air space in which to roll or spiral, and could only break away in horizontal flight. As he swung out of a turn Yonekawa was on him in a flash. There was no question of his accuracy this time. The P-39 dropped into the jungle and disappeared.'

A flight of A6M2s run up their Nakajima Sakae radial engines before taking off. Delivering under 1000 hp, it was less powerful than many contemporary fighter engines in Germany, Britain and the USA, but the Zero was so light its lack of power did not become a handicap until later in the war. (*via Chris Bishop*)

Zero versus Mustang

One of the newest American fighters, the North American P-51 Mustang, was much more evenly matched, and in several respects was clearly superior to the Zero.

'The P-51 was drawing 3000 rpm and 43 inches manifold pressure for its take-off and climb to 5000 feet. The low manifold pressure was due to the automatic manifold pressure regulator. The Zero left the ground and reached its best climb speed approximately six seconds before the P-51. At 5000 feet from a cruising speed of 250 mph (217 kt) indicated, the P-51 accelerated sharply away from the Zero. Climb from 5000 to 10,000, and from 10,000 to 15,000 feet produced the same results, having the Zero accelerate away from the P-51 in rate of climb. At 10,000 feet from a cruising speed of 250 mph

(217 kt) indicated, the Mustang moved sharply away from the Zero, and at 15,000 feet from a cruising speed of 240 mph (208 kt) indicated the P-51 had the advantage over the Zero, but slightly slower than at 5000 and 10,000 feet. The P-51 could dive away from the Zero at any time. During this test, the P-51's powerplant failed to operate properly above 15,000 feet so the comparison was not continued above this altitude.'

It should be noted that this trial involved a P-51A Mustang, whose Allison engine was notoriously unreliable at altitude. Later, when P-51D Mustangs fitted with the splendid Packard-built Rolls-Royce Merlin engine reached the Pacific theatre, their superiority over the Zero was unquestioned.

The captured Zero was also flown against a

Captured Zeros are shipped to the United States on the deck of a US Navy aircraft carrier. One of the problems encountered in maintaining the Zero in an intact state was the lightweight metal used in its construction, which was affected by corrosion much more seriously then heavier alloys. (*via J.R. Cavanagh*)

Curtiss P-40F Tomahawk, but the tests were never completed because of problems with the USAAF fighter's Allison engine. Comparative trials with the Chance Vought F4U-1 Corsair, on the other hand, produced an illuminating and encouraging report.

'The Zero is far inferior to the F4U-1 in level and diving speeds at all altitudes. It falls short in climbs starting at sea level, and also above 20,000 feet. Between 5000 and 19,000 feet the situation varies. With slightly more than the normal fighter load, which may be distributed to give equal range and gun power, the Zero is slightly superior in average maximum rate of climb. This superiority becomes negligible at altitudes where carburettor air temperatures in the F4U are down to normal; close to the blower shift points it is more noticeable.

However, the Zero can not stay with the Corsair in high speed climbs. The superiority of the F4U at 30,000 feet is very evident, and would persist when carrying heavy loads.

Corsair's advantage

'In combat with the Zero, the Corsair can take full advantage of its speed along with its ability to pushover and roll at high speed if surprised. Due to its much higher wing loading, the F4U has to avoid any attempt to turn with the Zero unless at high speed, and can expect the latter to outclimb the Corsair at moderate altitudes and low airspeeds. In this case, the F4U should be climbed at high airspeed and on a heading which would open the distance and prevent the Zero from reaching a favourable position for diving attacks. After reaching 19,000 to 20,000

The North American P-51A Mustang could hold its own against the Zero, even though its Allison engine was poor at altitude. The Merlin-engined P-51D, seen here, was more than a match for the Zero. P-51Ds operating from Iwo Jima roved at will over southern Japan in the closing months of the war in the Pacific. (*Philip Jarrett*)

The A6M5 entered service at the same time as the Merlin Mustang. However, the Japanese fighter offered little improvement in performance over earlier models, though it had many more protective features. The Mustang, by contrast, was 100 mph faster than the fighters with which America had entered the war. (*via Chris Bishop*)

feet, the Corsair has superior performance in climb and can choose its own position for attack.'

Having proved its value beyond measure in teaching the Allies its capabilities, Tadayoshi Koga's Zero met an unfortunate end. In June 1944, a Curtiss Helldiver taxied into it at NAS North Island and chewed up its rear fuselage so badly that it was assessed as a total loss and scrapped. By that time, however, the offensive in New Guinea had enabled the Allies to capture examples of a later model, the A6M3 Zero Model 32, and comparative tests continued with these aircraft.

One of the biggest shocks to the Allies, at least initially, was the ability of the Zero to get the better of the Supermarine Spitfire, an aircraft that had achieved almost legendary status thanks to its prowess in the Battle of Britain. The Zero vs. Spitfire episode is worth examining in detail.

On 19 February 1942, the Japanese 1st Carrier Air Fleet launched a devastating attack on the North Australian harbour of Port Darwin. Escorted by 36 Zeros, 71 dive-bombers and 81 torpedo-bombers swept down on the port, destroying the American warship USS *Peary*, seven merchant vessels and four small harbour vessels. It was the first of a series of heavy air attacks directed against Darwin and other strategic targets in northern Australia during 1942.

Throughout that year, the air defence of northern Australia was the responsibility of the 49th Fighter Group, USAAF, equipped with P-40E Kittyhawks, which was joined after

The Chance Vought F4U Corsair outclassed the Zero in every respect except manoeuvrability. Seen here is a Corsair of Navy Fighter Squadron VF-17, flown by Lt Ira Kepford, the fifth-ranking US Navy ace of WWII. Note the 16 Japanese flags denoting kills under the cockpit. Kepford's final score was 17. (*Philip Jarrett*)

August by Nos 76 and 77 Squadrons RAAF, also armed with this type. As the P-40 was no match for the Zero, the Australian Government urgently requested a shipment of Spitfires from the UK, and after a lengthy delay three Spitfire squadrons – No. 54 RAF and Nos 452 and 457 RAAF – were established in the Darwin area in mid-January 1943, together with their radar-equipped Mobile Fighter Sector HQ. The three squadrons together formed No. 1 Fighter Wing, which was led by Wing Commander Clive Caldwell, a highly experienced and skilled fighter pilot with 20 victories to his credit in North Africa.

In February 1943 the Japanese renewed their bombing offensive against northern Australia, and on the 6th of that month Flt Lt R.W. Foster opened the Spitfire's scoreboard in the theatre by shooting down a Mitsubishi Ki 46 'Dinah' reconnaissance aircraft 35 miles WNW of Cape Van Dieman. It was a good start, because so far the 'Dinahs' had been able to operate with near impunity, their speed and ceiling making them virtually immune to interception by fighters such as the P-40. The arrival of the Spitfire – and the Lockheed P-38F, which was now being deployed by the Americans – changed that situation.

Spitfire V outclassed

It remained to be seen how the tropicalised Spitfire VC would perform against the Zero. The pilots were confident that whatever performance shortcomings the Spitfire might have when confronted by the Japanese fighter – and by now the Allies knew just how well the

P-40s of the 49th Fighter Group were originally responsible for the air defence of northern Australia. The group was joined in August 1942 by Nos 76 and 77 Squadrons RAAF, also equipped with P-40s. The heavy Curtiss fighter was no match for the Zero in a dogfight: its only advantage was its superior diving speed. (*USAF*)

A6M performed – they would be levelled out by superior skill and tactics. This confidence seemed to be justified when, during a raid on Coomalie by 16 Nakajima B5N 'Kate' torpedo-bombers with a fighter escort on 2 March, the Spitfires claimed two Zeros and a 'Kate' for no loss. On 23 March Darwin was subjected to its 53rd air attack, during which 21 bombers and 24 escorting Zeros were intercepted by the whole of No. 1 Fighter Wing. In the air battle that developed over the harbour the Spitfires shot down three Zeros and four Mitsubishi G4M 'Betty' bombers, but three Spitfires were lost.

There were no raids on the Darwin area in April 1943, but at 09.26 on Sunday 2 May, an incoming Japanese force was detected by radar while it was still a long way out to sea – 49 minutes' flying time from the coast, in fact –

and the Wing's 33 Spitfires were all airborne within 15 minutes. The enemy formation, comprising 18 bombers and 27 fighters, was sighted when the Spitfires were at 7000 m (23,000 ft). Since the Japanese were still about 1200 m (nearly 4000 ft) higher, Caldwell knew that to attack them on the climb would be suicidal, for the nimble Zeros would have all the advantages. He delayed the attack and continued to climb while the Spitfires got into position above the enemy, with the glare of the sun behind them.

At 10.15 the Japanese flew over Darwin and bombed the harbour unmolested while the Spitfires were still trying to get into position. After completing their bombing run the enemy altered course and crossed the coast, losing height gradually as they increased speed. The

The Mk VC Spitfire, which could be easily out-manoeuvred by the Zero, was eventually replaced by the Mk VIII, which performed well at both high and low level and which also saw action in Burma. This example is seen in South East Asia Command insignia. (*Philip Jarrett*)

Spitfires were now at 9750 m (nearly 32,000 ft) and were behind the Japanese formation.

Bitter lesson

Caldwell's fighters shadowed the Japanese until they were out over the Timor Sea, then he ordered No. 54 Squadron to attack the Zeros while the other two squadrons engaged the bombers. The Spitfires, now with the advantage of height, went into the attack almost vertically at 650 km/h (400 mph). A furious air battle developed as the Zero pilots, recovering from their surprise, turned to meet the attackers. It was now that the Spitfire pilots learned a bitter lesson. The lightly built Zero, with its high power-weight ratio, could out-turn the Spitfire VC with ease. It could also perform some extraordinary manoeuvres that the pilot of anything but a Zero would never dare attempt in the middle of a dogfight. For example, one experienced Australian pilot was making a shallow diving attack on a Zero when the enemy fighter suddenly performed a tight loop that brought it on to the tail of the Australian,

who narrowly avoided being shot down.

When the battle was over, five Zeros had been shot down, but only one bomber; and on the debit side five Spitfires had been lost in combat, two of the pilots being killed, while five more had to make emergency landings because of fuel starvation and another three because of engine failure. The Australian popular press was scathing in its criticism.

By the end of May 1943 No. 1 Fighter Wing had destroyed 24 enemy aircraft for the loss of ten Spitfires in combat. Other Spitfires, though, were lost in forced landings; the Merlin engines were suffering badly from wear and tear, and replacements were non-existent. During high-altitude actions problems were experienced with the Spitfires' 20-mm cannon, the freezing conditions causing malfunction and jamming. Even if only one cannon jammed, the recoil from the other caused the aircraft to yaw so that the aim was spoiled.

Ignoring the growing storm of criticism about the famous Spitfire's lack of success, Caldwell continued to refine the Fighter Wing's

Mitsubishi A6M2 Zero Model 11, equipped with a long-range fuel tank, pictured over China while operating with the 12th Air Group Fighter Squadron. The Zero destroyed its first enemy aircraft on 13 September 1940. Reports of its performance were ignored by the RAF, which at that time was embroiled in the Battle of Britain. Its superior agility came as a shock to the first Spitfire pilots who encountered it. (*via J.R. Cavanagh*)

tactics, confident that the situation was about to change. It did, on 20 June 1943.

That morning, Darwin radar detected enemy aircraft approaching, and within minutes 46 Spitfires were airborne. A short time later, the pilots of Nos 54 and 452 Squadrons, climbing hard, sighted 25 Japanese bombers over Bathurst Island, escorted by a similar number of Zeros. The enemy, at 8540 m (28,000 ft), were slightly lower than the two Spitfire squadrons, which immediately launched their attack. No. 54 Squadron destroyed seven bombers and a Zero, while No. 452 shot down three bombers and one fighter.

Improved results

The enemy formation altered course towards Darwin, where No. 457 Squadron shot down a 'Betty'. After releasing their bombs the enemy flew across Darwin harbour, losing another two Zeros. Meanwhile, ten more bombers had made a low-level attack on Darwin airfield without fighter opposition, but as they withdrew they were intercepted by No. 54 Squadron, which destroyed another bomber. During the morning's engagements the Fighter Wing lost only two Spitfires, both of No. 452 Squadron. Against 12 bombers and four fighters destroyed, it was not a bad balance sheet. For once, the critics were silenced.

On 30 June, 27 'Bettys' escorted by 23 Zeros attacked Long and Fenton airfields, from where US Fifth Air Force B-24 bombers had just begun a series of heavy attacks on Japanese bases in the Celebes. In the course of a running battle with the Spitfires, the Japanese lost six 'Bettys' and three Zeros; four Spitfires were written off, three as a result of engine failure.

By now, the Merlin engines were so worn out that when the Fighter Wing put up 36 aircraft to intercept 47 Japanese bombers and fighters, only seven managed to engage the enemy. The rest either failed to reach altitude or were forced to return early with engine problems. Nevertheless, the seven that did engage displayed superb tactical skill, destroying seven 'Bettys' and two Zeros. Eight Spitfires were written off, mostly in forced landings.

On 7 September 1943 radar detected an incoming Japanese formation about 180 miles (290 km) out to sea. Forty-eight Spitfires were scrambled to intercept the enemy, which turned out to be a lone 'Dinah' reconnaissance aircraft escorted by 20 Zeros. The latter 'bounced' No. 54 Squadron and shot down three Spitfires. The other No. 54 Squadron pilots destroyed one Zero and damaged two more, while four other Zeros were shot down by the other pilots of the Wing. This marked the end of Japanese attempts to penetrate the Darwin area by

The last mark of Spitfire to see action against the Japanese was the Griffon-engined Mk XIV, but by the time it arrived in the Far East the war was virtually over. Nearly 100 mph faster than the Zero, it was used by several squadrons of the Indian Air Force from February 1945 until the early 1950s. (*Philip Jarrett*)

daylight; they now switched to sporadic night attacks which continued, with little effect, until early in 1944. Caldwell's Spitfires had fulfilled their task, albeit with far greater losses than had been anticipated.

Zero in Burma

In Burma, RAF Spitfires began to encounter increasing numbers of A6M3 Zero Model 32 aircraft from the beginning of 1944. These aircraft served alongside the Nakajima Ki.43 Hayabusa (Oscar) in mixed fighter units, notably the 21st, 33rd, 50th and 64th Air Regiments of the Japanese Army Air Force. In the closing months of the war, the Spitfire's naval counterpart, the Seafire, also saw action against the Zero while serving aboard the carriers of the British Pacific Fleet. In this case, most of the Zeros encountered were engaged in *kamikaze* suicide missions.

Testing captured examples of the A6M3 and its successor, the A6M5 Model 52, produced a new crop of evaluation assessments. The first A6M5 fell into Allied hands in June 1944,

following the capture of Saipan in the Marianas, and like the preceding captured models was tested exhaustively. Following comparison between the Grumman F6F Hellcat and the A6M5, the report stated that:

'The Zero climbs about 600 ft/min better than the F6F up to 9000 feet, after which the advantage falls off gradually until the two aircraft are about equal at 14,000 feet. Above this altitude the Hellcat has the advantage, varying from 500 ft/min better at 22,000 feet, to about 250 ft/min better at 30,000 feet.

'Best climb speeds of the F6F-5 and the Zero 52 are 150 mph (130 kt) and 122 mph (105 kt) indicated, respectively. The F6F-5 is faster than the Zero 52 at all altitudes, having the least margin of 25 mph (21.5 kt) at 5000 feet and the widest difference of 57 mph (65 kt) at 25,000 feet. Top speeds attained were 409 mph (355 kt) at 21,600 feet for the Hellcat, and 335 mph (290 kt) at 18,000 feet for the Zero.'

Comparative testing between the A6M5 and the Vought F4U-1D Corsair revealed that:

'In a race for altitude, the best climb of the

While late marks of Zero, like these A6M5s seen at Oita in August 1944, retained all of the type's agility, their performance suffered by comparison with Allied contemporaries. Japan did develop advanced fighters, but American bombing meant that production was limited and the Zero had to soldier on. (*via Chris Bishop*)

F4U-1D is equal to the Zero up to 10,000 feet, above 750 ft/min better at 18,000 feet and above 500 ft/min better at 22,000 feet and above. Best climb speeds of the F4U and Zero are 156 mph (135 kt) and 122 mph (105 kt) indicated airspeed, respectively. The F4U-1D is faster than the Zero 52 at all altitudes, having the least margin of 42 mph (37.5 kt) at 5000 feet and the widest difference of 80 mph (70 kt) at 25,000 feet. Top speeds attained were 413 mph (360 kt) TAS at 20,400 feet for the Corsair and 335 mph (290 kt) TAS at 18,000 feet for the Zero.

'Rate of roll for the Zero was equal to that of the Corsair at speeds under 230 mph (200 kt) and inferior above that speed due to the high control forces. Manoeuvrability of the Zero is remarkable at speeds below 202 mph (175 kt), being far superior to that of the Corsair. In slow speed turns the Zero can gain one turn in three and a half at 10,000 feet. At speeds around 202 mph (175 kt), however, the F4U can, by using flaps, stay with the Zero for about one-half turn, or until its speed fell off to 173 mph (150 kt). Initial dive accelerations of the Zero and the Corsair are about the same after which the Corsair is far superior, and slightly superior in zooms after dives.'

Dire pilot shortage

Although the latest American fighter types were better in terms of all-round performance than the Zero, it was the dire shortage of skilled pilots that stripped away Japanese air superiority in the Pacific. In the hands of one of the dwindling band of Japanese aces, the Mitsubishi fighter could still show its quality, as

The fate of many of the Imperial Japanese Navy's Zero force was to be left behind as wreckage when the tide of Allied advances swept over the island outposts of the Empire. This A6M2 was recovered almost intact at Buna as Australian and American troops worked their way along the northern coast of New Guinea. (*via Chris Bishop*)

one leading US fighter pilot discovered to his cost in a dogfight.

On 7 December 1944, the third anniversary of the Japanese attack on Pearl Harbor, the US Fifth Air Force's 475th Fighter Group, equipped with Lockheed P-38 Lightnings, destroyed 28 enemy aircraft over the Philippines. Two of them were shot down by Major Tommy McGuire, commanding the 431st Squadron. McGuire was the second-ranking American ace, close behind the leading fighter pilot, Major Richard Bong. On 26 December, McGuire shot down four Zeros, bringing his score to 38 – only two short of Richard Bong's total of 40 aircraft destroyed.

On 7 January, 1945, Tommy McGuire was leading a patrol of four Lightnings on an offensive mission against the enemy airfield at Los Negros when a lone Zero was sighted. The Lightnings dived on the tail of the enemy, whose pilot calmly waited until they were almost within range – then at the last moment throwing his aircraft into a very tight left-handed turn they could not follow. It brought him onto the tail of Lt Rittmeyer, McGuire's wingman. A short burst of fire, and Rittmeyer's P-38 went down in flames.

The Zero continued to turn easily inside the other three Lightnings, and in an effort to get at the Japanese pilot McGuire attempted too tight a turn at low speed. The P-38 stalled and plunged into the jungle below. The other two Lightnings broke off the engagement, leaving the Zero to continue unmolested on its way.

1. Zero Family: Versions and Variants

Mitsubishi *12-Shi* Fighter

The designation A6M1 was allocated by the Imperial Japanese Navy to the prototype Zero, the *12-Shi* Fighter, when the latter was accepted for service at the end of July 1940. It was also allocated to the second aircraft, both machines being powered by the 875-hp Mitsubishi Zuisei (Holy Star) 13 engine.

A6M1 Specification
Powerplant: one 875-hp Mitsubishi Zuisei 13 14-cylinder radial
Max speed: 508 km/h (316 mph) at 3600 m (11,800 ft)
Time to height: 7 min 15 sec to 5000 m (16,400 ft)
Service ceiling: 10,000 m (32,810 ft)
Max range: not known
Wing span: 12.00 m (39 ft 4 in)
Length: 9.06 m (29ft 8 in)
Height: 3.05 m (10 ft)
Weights: 1680 kg (3704 lb) empty, 2343 kg (5155 lb) loaded
Armament: two 20-mm Type 99 (Oerlikon) fixed forward-firing cannon in wing leading edges; two fixed forward-firing 7.7-mm machine-guns in forward fuselage; external bomb load of 120 kg (265 lb)

A6M2 Model 11/21

The designation A6M2 Model 11 was applied to the third prototype, which was powered by the 950-hp Nakajima NK1C Sakae 12 engine. An initial batch of 15 pre-production aircraft was deployed to China with the 12th Air Group Fighter Squadron. The Zero destroyed its first enemy aircraft on 13 September 1940.

As experience with the pre-production aircraft built up, several modifications were introduced on the production line, the first being a reinforcement of the rear spar introduced on the 22nd A6M2. Sixty-four A6M2 Model 11s were built; beginning with the 65th aircraft, folding wingtips were incorporated to provide adequate deck elevator clearance for shipboard operations, and with this modification the type was designated A6M2 Model 21. Starting with the 127th aircraft, new aileron balance tabs were fitted to give better response at all speed ranges.

Total production of the A6M2 Model 21, which was built by both Mitsubishi and Nakajima, was 740 machines, the fighter being known to the Allies as the 'Zeke 21'.

A6M2 Specification
Powerplant: one 950-hp Nakajima NK1C Sakae 12 14-cylinder radial
Max speed: 534 km/h (332 mph) at 4500 m (14,930 ft)
Time to height: 5 min 50 sec to 5000 m (16,400 ft)
Service ceiling: 10,300 m (33,780 ft)
Max range: 3105 km (1930 miles)
Wing span: 12.00 m (39 ft 4 in)
Length: 9.06 m (29 ft 8 in)
Height: 3.05 m (10 ft)
Weights: 1680 kg (3704 lb) empty, 2343 kg (5155 lb) loaded
Armament: As A6M1

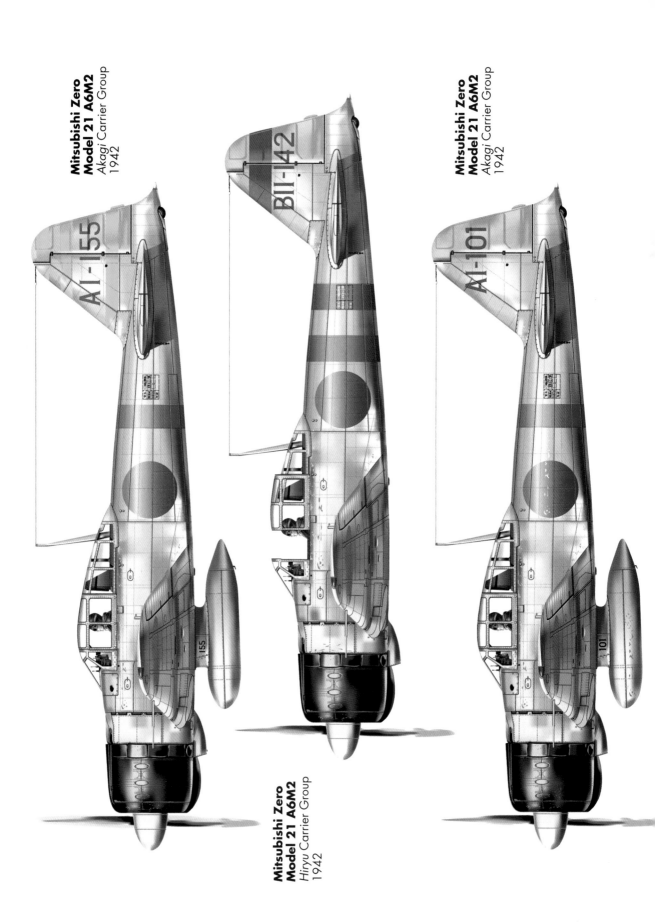

Mitsubishi Zero
Model 21 A6M2
Akagi Carrier Group
1942

Mitsubishi Zero
Model 21 A6M2
Akagi Carrier Group
1942

Mitsubishi Zero
Model 21 A6M2
Hiryu Carrier Group
1942

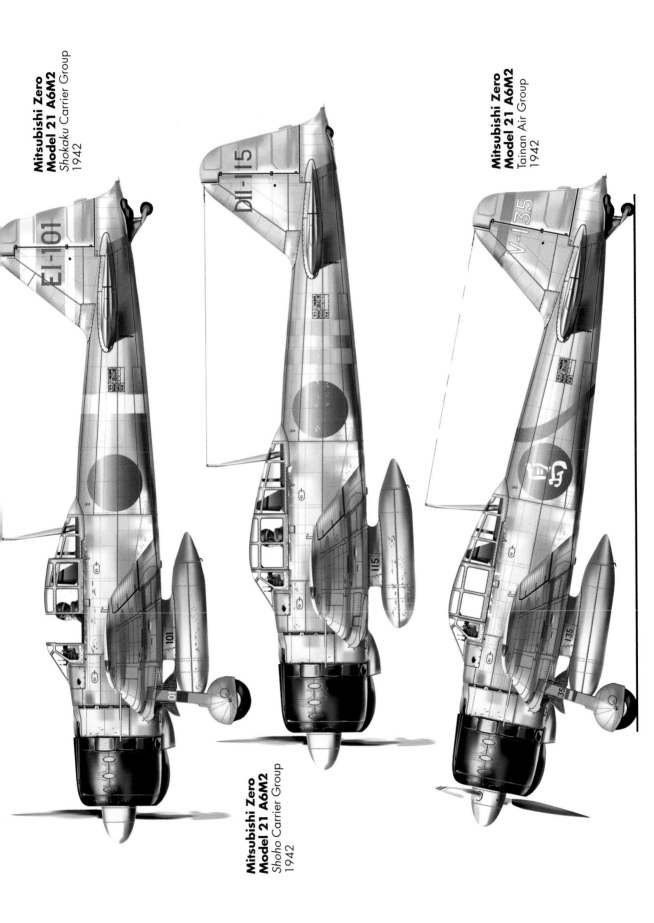

Mitsubishi Zero
Model 21 A6M2
Shokaku Carrier Group
1942

Mitsubishi Zero
Model 21 A6M2
Tainan Air Group
1942

Mitsubishi Zero
Model 21 A6M2
Shoho Carrier Group
1942

A6M3 Model 32

Six months before the outbreak of the Pacific War, Mitsubishi began testing a new version of the Zero. The A6M3 was powered by an 1130-hp Sakae 21 14-cylinder radial fitted with a two-stage supercharger. Installation of the new engine meant that the firewall had to be moved 20.3 cm (8 in) aft, resulting in a reduction in fuselage fuel tank capacity from 98 litres (21.6 Imp gal) to 60 litres (13.2 Imp gal). The shape of the engine cowling was also changed to incorporate a scoop-type supercharger air intake in the upper lip.

Despite the increase in engine power, there was no spectacular increase in performance; in fact, although fuel consumption at normal cruising speed was about the same as the Sakae12's, consumption at combat power was much higher, and this, together with the reduction in combat radius, caused many A6M3 losses through fuel starvation.

As a means of improving the aircraft's maximum speed, the folding wingtips were removed, giving the A6M3 a more angular appearance than the A6M2, so that when the variant was first encountered over the Solomon Islands in October 1942 the Allies believed that it was a new type and accordingly gave it a new code-name.

The initial choice was 'Hap', which was the nickname of USAAF General H.H. Arnold; he was not amused, and so the name was changed to 'Hamp'. It was not until December 1942, when the Americans had an opportunity to examine an A6M3 at close quarters in New Guinea, that they realized it was nothing more than a modification of the basic Zero design, and so the code-name was again altered, this time to 'Zeke 32'.

The reduction in wing area made the A6M3 slightly more agile at high speeds. As a further improvement, the 20-mm ammunition load was increased from 60 to 100 rounds per gun.

If the A6M3's square-cut appearance had confused the Allies, there was further confusion when, late in 1942, it turned up over New Guinea and the Solomon Islands sporting rounded wingtips once more. This was the result of a decision by Mitsubishi, following approaches from operational units, to fit a 45-litre (9.9-Imp gal) fuel tank in each wing

outboard of the cannon bay, which meant restoring the folding wingtips to retain an acceptably low wing loading. In this new configuration the A6M3 became the Model 22. It had the longest range of all Zero variants – about 160 km (100 miles) more than the A6M2 – and it was capable of making the 1036-km (644-mile) round trip from Rabaul to the Guadalcanal battle area and back. Total production of the Model 32 and Model 22 Zero was 343 and 560 respectively.

A6M3 Model 32 Specification
Powerplant: one 1130-hp Nakajima NK1F Sakae 21 14-cylinder radial
Max speed: 544 km/h (338 mph) at 6000 m (19,685 ft)
Time to height: 7 min 19 sec to 6000 m (19,680 ft)
Service ceiling: 11,050 m (36,240 ft)
Max range: 2328 km (1447 miles)
Wing span: 11.00 m (36 ft 1 in)
Length: 9.06 m (29 ft 8 in)
Height: 3.50 m (11 ft 6 in)
Weights: 1807 kg (3884 lb) empty, 2544 kg (5609 lb) loaded
Armament: As A6M1

A6M5 Model 52

The A6M3 Model 22 had a relatively short operational life, thanks to the appearance of a new Zero variant. The new aircraft was the A6M5 Zero Model 52, known as 'Zeke 52' to the Allies. The missing A6M4 designation was reserved for a version of the A6M2 with a turbo-supercharged engine, but although this configuration was tested experimentally in two A6M2 airframes, it was not a success and there was never a production A6M4 Zero.

The A6M5 variant was developed because of the need to increase the Zero's diving speed, which by mid-1943 could not match that of the latest Allied fighters. A modified wing was the answer, and in August 1943 Mitsubishi fitted the 904th production A6M3 with a new set of wings featuring heavier gauge skin. The unused wingtip folding mechanism, which had been simply faired over when the A6M3's wingtip had been squared off, was eliminated and the tip rounded. The wing span remained the same as that of the A6M3.

The Mitsubishi A6M5 Zero Model 52 was the best of the Zero line. It was also the most widely used, 1701 examples being built in three sub-series. The type was rushed into service in the autumn of 1943 to counter the US Navy's Grumman F6F Hellcat, and served through until the end of the war. (*Philip Jarrett*)

Another modification designed to increase speed was the replacement of the engine exhaust collector ring with straight individual stacks, which provided some extra thrust augmentation. The overall result was an aircraft that weighed about 78 kg (170 lb) more than the A6M3, but with a maximum speed at 6000 m (19,685 ft) of 565 km/h (351 mph) against the A6M3's 544 km/h (338 mph). The aircraft could now be safely dived at up to 660 km/h (410 mph) without risking structural failure.

The A6M5 was the best and most widely used of the A6M series, 1701 examples being built in three sub-series. The first A6M5s were rushed into service in the autumn of 1943 to counter the Grumman F6F Hellcat, but it was soon apparent that the latter's fast-firing armament of six 0.50-in Browning heavy machine-guns, its stronger construction and better protection, combined to give the American fighter the edge over the A6M5 in combat.

The A6M5, which had entered production as the Navy Type 0 Carrier Fighter Model 52, retained the same armament as the A6M3 – two cannon and two machine-guns – but the cannon feed mechanism was now changed from drum to belt, making it possible to provide each 20-mm cannon with an extra 100 rounds. A wing skin of still heavier gauge was also fitted, enabling the diving speed to be increased to 740 km/h (460 mph). In this guise the aircraft was designated A6M5a Model 52a. Production, which was shared between Mitsubishi and Nakajima, began in March 1944.

A6M5b

With the next sub-variant, the A6M5b, the Japanese at last woke up to the fact that protection, both for the pilot and for vital parts of the aircraft, was an important factor in combat survival. This sub-variant, which was jointly developed by Mitsubishi and Dai-Ichi Kaigun Kokusho, featured an automatic CO_2 fire extinguisher system built into the fuel tank areas of the fuselage and around the engine firewall, while a 50-mm (2-in) bullet-proof windshield was fitted to give the pilot some forward protection. Thanks to the extraordinary Japanese mentality that continued to prevail at the time, there was still no rear protection for the pilot; the notion that a Japanese pilot might

73

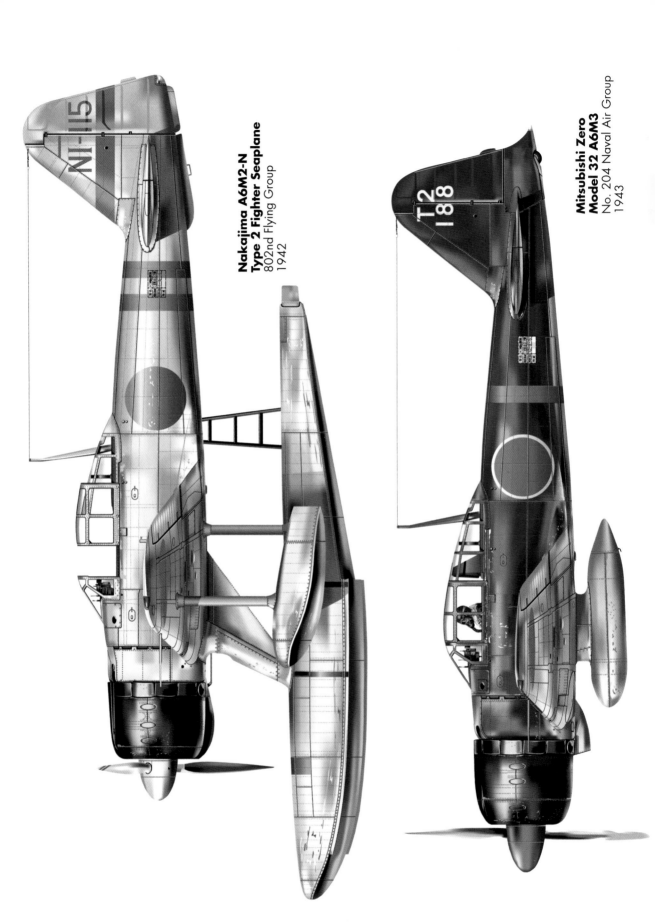

**Nakajima A6M2-N
Type 2 Fighter Seaplane**
802nd Flying Group
1942

**Mitsubishi Zero
Model 32 A6M3**
No. 204 Naval Air Group
1943

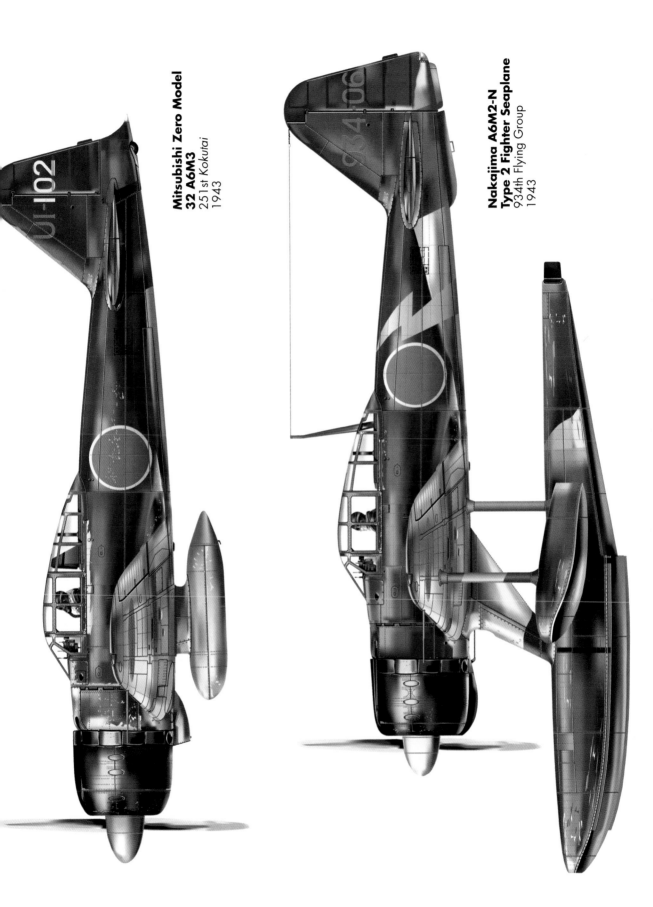

**Mitsubishi Zero Model
32 A6M3**
251st Kokutai
1943

**Nakajima A6M2-N
Type 2 Fighter Seaplane**
934th Flying Group
1943

need to run away was inconceivable.

Firepower was also increased in the A6M5b, one of the two fuselage-mounted 7.7-mm machine-guns being replaced by a heavier 13-mm weapon. Despite these improvements, Imperial Japanese Navy fighter units equipped with the A6M5 (which were the majority) suffered massive losses during the battle for the Philippines in the latter half of 1944. Many aircraft were fitted with a 550-lb (250-kg) bomb and expended in *kamikaze* attacks.

Development of the land-based partner of the Zero, the Mitsubishi J2M *Raiden* (Thunderbolt), was far behind schedule, and although production was under way it was painfully slow. Mitsubishi, therefore, had no choice but to continue producing the Zero in order to meet the ever more pressing demands of the Navy.

A6M5c

In July 1944 a top priority modification programme resulted in the A6M5c, a sub-variant which, for the first time, incorporated armour plate behind the pilot's seat and armoured glass in the rear canopy panels.

The armament was again increased, a wing-mounted 13-mm machine-gun being added outboard of each 20-mm cannon. To compensate for some of the inevitable weight increase, the 7.7-mm nose gun was removed. To increase the A6M5's range, a 140-litre (30-Imp gal) self-sealing fuel tank was installed behind the cockpit; and to increase the fighter's chances of destroying the Boeing B-29 Superfortresses which were beginning to attack Japan from bases in China, underwing racks for small unguided air-to-air missiles were fitted. These missiles were to have been modelled on the German R4M, but as far as it is known they were never used.

A6M5 Specification
Powerplant: one 1130-hp Nakajima NK1F Sakae 21 14-cylinder radial
Max speed: 565 km/h (351 mph) at 6000 m (19,685 ft)
Time to height: 7 min 1 sec to 6000 m (19,680 ft)
Service ceiling: 11,050 m (36,240 ft)
Max range: 1194 miles (1921 km)
Wing span: 11.00 m (36 ft 1 in)

Length: 9.12 m (29 ft 11 in)
Height: 3.50 m (11 ft 6 in)
Weights: 1876 kg (4136 lb) empty, 2733 kg (6025 lb) loaded
Armament: A6M5 as A6M1; (A6M5b) one 7.7-mm and one 13.2-mm MG in the upper fuselage decking, and two wing-mounted 20-mm cannon; (A6M5c) one 13.2-mm machine-gun in upper fuselage decking, two wing-mounted 13.2-mm machine-guns and two wing-mounted 20-mm cannon

A6M6c Model 53c

For some time, the Mitsubishi engineering team, now led by Eitaro Sano (Jiro Horikoshi having moved on to the design of a new advanced fighter, the A7M *Reppu*) had been recommending the replacement of the Zero's Sakae 21 engine with the 1350-hp Mitsubishi Kinsei 62. The Navy refused to sanction this on the grounds that the engines were needed for other types and that in any case it would take too long to adapt the new powerplant to the Zero airframe.

As an alternative, the Navy suggested using water-methanol injection to provide emergency boost for the existing Sakae engine, and in November 1944 Mitsubishi installed an experimental water-methanol powerplant, designated Sakae 31a, in a Zero airframe. Production aircraft, designated A6M6c, were to be fitted with self-sealing fuel tanks. In the event, persistent trouble with the engine and development problems with the self-sealing tanks caused the project to be abandoned, and only one prototype was built. Performance details have not been recorded.

A6M7 Model 63

The A6M7 Zero stemmed from an urgent requirement, originating in the summer of 1944, for a fighter/dive-bomber possessing enough speed and manoeuvrability to break through increasingly strong enemy defences and reach its target. Some operational units had already carried out a local modification of the Zero's belly tank attachment, enabling it to carry a 250-kg (550-lb) bomb, but this arrangement was unreliable and the Navy instructed Mitsubishi to design a more efficient bomb rack. Production of the modified aircraft began in May 1945, most being expended as *kamikazes*.

Rulers of the skies no more...derelict Zeros were scattered all over the Pacific and Southeast Asia after the end of the war. Many of the aircraft had been hurriedly painted with green-and-white surrender insignia. Once the Emperor ordered Japan to surrender, the will to go on resisting collapsed. (*Harry Holmes*)

A6M7 Specification

Powerplant: one 1560-hp Nakajima Sakae 31 14-cylinder radial
Max speed: 542 km/h (337 mph) at 6400 m (20,992 ft)
Time to height: 7 min 58 sec to 6000 m (19,680 ft)
Service ceiling: 10,180 m (33,390 ft)
Max range: 1517 km (943 miles)
Wing span: 11.00 m (36 ft 1 in)
Length: 9.12 m (29 ft 11 in)
Height: 3.50 m (11 ft 6 in)
Weights: 1876 kg (4136 lb) empty, 2733 kg (3000 lb) loaded
Armament: As A6M5c, but modified to carry one 250-kg (550-lb) bomb

A6M8 Model 64

By November 1944, the supply of Nakajima Sakae engines was beginning to dry up, partly because production had switched to the new Homare engine that was to power the Mitsubishi A7M1 *Reppu* fighter. The Navy consequently agreed to the installation of Mitsubishi Kinsei 62 engines in new-build Zeros, a move which had been advocated years before by Jiro Horikoshi.

The forward fuselage was redesigned to accommodate the larger and more powerful engine, the fuselage-mounted gun being deleted; other changes included the removal of the fuel tanks' self-sealing material, which was replaced by the earlier fire extinguisher system used in the A6M5b, and an increase in fuel capacity to permit two and a half hours' flying time at normal cruise. Two A6M8 prototypes were built, the first being accepted by the Navy on 25 May, 1945. The aircraft's performance was impressive enough to warrant an order for 6300 production aircraft, but none could be completed before the end of the war.

A6M8 Specification

Powerplant: one 1560-hp Mitsubishi MK8P Kinsei 62 14-cylinder radial
Max speed: 573 km/h (356 mph) at 6000 m (19,685 ft)
Time to height: 6 min 50 sec to 6000 m

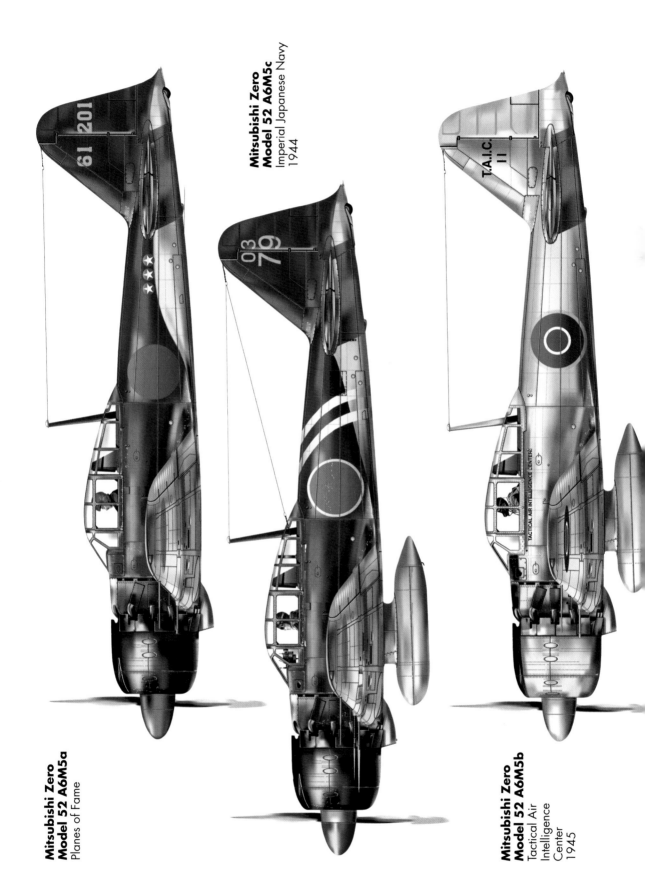

**Mitsubishi Zero
Model 52 A6M5a**
Planes of Fame

**Mitsubishi Zero
Model 52 A6M5c**
Imperial Japanese Navy
1944

**Mitsubishi Zero
Model 52 A6M5b**
Tactical Air
Intelligence
Center
1945

T.A.I.C.
II

TACTICAL AIR INTELLIGENCE CENTER

Mitsubishi Zero
Model 21 A6M2
Allied Tactical
Air Intelligence Unit
1945

BI-12

ATAIU SEA

Mitsubishi Zero
Model 52 A6M5b
Tactical Air
Intelligence Center
1945

T.A.I.C.
8

TACTICAL AIR INTELLIGENCE CENTER

Mitsubishi Zero
Model 52 A6M5c
Japanese surrender markings
1945

The A6M2-K, built by Nakajima, was the first two-seat Zero trainer conversion. The A6M2-K was extensively operated in Japan and Formosa, and in addition to its primary training mission it was used for target towing. Some were expended in *kamikaze* attacks at the end of the war. (*Philip Jarrett*)

Service ceiling: 11,200 m (37,075 ft)
Max range: 1517 km (943 miles)
Wing span: 11.0 m (36 ft 1 in)
Length: 9.23 m (30 ft 3 in)
Height: 3.63 m (11 ft 11 in)
Weights: 2150 kg (4740 lb) empty, 3150 kg (6945 lb) loaded
Armament: two wing-mounted 13.2-mm machine-guns and two 20-mm cannon

A6M2-K trainer

Completed in November 1943, the A6M2-K was a two-seat trainer conversion of the A6M2. To compensate for the weight of the student pilot, the two wing-mounted 20-mm cannon were removed. The Sakae 12 engine was retained. Development of a similar two-seat trainer based on the A6M5 was begun in August 1944, but only seven A6M5-Ks were completed.

A6M2-K Specification

Crew: 2
Powerplant: one 950-hp Nakajima NK1C Sakae 12 14-cylinder radial
Max speed: 476 km/h (296 mph) at 4000 m (13,125 ft)
Time to height: 7 min 56 sec to 6000 m (19,680 ft)
Service ceiling: 10,180 m (33,400 ft)

Max range: 1384 km (860 miles)
Wing span: 12.0 m (39 ft 4in)
Length: 9.15 m (30 ft 0 in)
Height: 3.53 m (11 ft 7 in)
Weights: 1819 kg (4010 lb) empty, 2334 kg (5146 lb) loaded
Armament: two 7.7-mm fuselage-mounted machine-guns

Nakajima A6M2-N

Code-named 'Rufe' by the Allies, the Nakajima A6M2-N was a floatplane fighter adaptation of the Mitsubishi A6M2 Zero and was intended for operations from water bases among the scattered Pacific atolls. The project was assigned to the Nakajima company, who completed 327 aircraft between April 1942 and September 1943, the prototype flying on 8 December 1941. The A6M2-N was first encountered during the battle for the Solomons. The type was used mainly for home defence and reconnaissance, although it was occasionally encountered in its fighter role in the Aleutian Islands, at Guadalcanal and over the Bay of Bengal. The A6M2-N, despite its large float, was fast and manoeuvrable. Units equipped with the type included the Yokosuka, Yokohama, Otsu, 5th, 36th and 452nd Kokutais (Naval Air Corps).

Code-named 'Rufe' by the Allies, the A6M2-N floatplane version of the Zero was built by Nakajima. After flying the prototype for the first time in December 1941, Nakajima built 327 production A6M2-Ns in their Koizumi plant between April 1942 and September 1943. *(Harry Holmes)*

A6M2-N Specification

Powerplant: one 950-hp Nakajima NK1C Sakae 12 14-cylinder radial
Max speed: 434 km/h (270 mph) at 5000 m (16,405 ft)
Time to height: 6 min 43 sec to 5000 m (16,405 ft)
Service ceiling: 10,180 m (33,400 ft)
Max range: 1781 km (1107 miles)
Wing span: 12.0 m (39 ft 4 in)
Length: 10.1 m (33 ft 1 in)
Height: 4.3 m (14 ft 1 in)
Weights: 1912 kg (4235 lb) empty, 2460 kg (5423 lb) loaded
Armament: As A6M1

ZERO CONTEMPORARIES AND SUCCESSORS:

Mitsubishi J2M

Development of the Mitsubishi J2M *Raiden* (Thunderbolt) began in October 1938, in response to an Imperial Japanese Navy requirement for a land-based interceptor. The project was shelved for nearly a year while designer Jiro Horikoshi and his team concentrated on the ongoing development of the Zero fighter. The first of three J2M prototypes flew on 20 March 1942, and after some necessary modifications the type was ordered into production in October that year. However, constant problems were experienced

Started at roughly the same time as the A6M, the Mitsubishi J2M *Raiden* (Allied code-name 'Jack') was intended to be the Imperial Japanese Navy's standard land-based interceptor, but its development was delayed considerably because of preoccupation with the A6M. The prototype did not fly until March 1942. (*Philip Jarrett*)

with the Kasei 23a, the first Japanese-developed engine with water-methanol injection, and by March 1943 only 14 J2Ms had been delivered, including the prototypes.

Known to the Allies as 'Jack', the type was used almost exclusively for home defence, although some were encountered during the Marianas campaign in September 1944. Probably the best variant was the J2M5, which had its armament reduced to two 20-mm cannon. Its excellent rate of climb made it an ideal high-altitude interceptor, but supply shortages of its Kasei 26a engine resulted in only 35 being built out of a total of about 500. In fact, production of the *Raiden* was slowed down in the summer of 1944 because of the priority given to the other land-based Navy fighter, the Kawanishi N1K *Shiden*.

J2M Specification
Powerplant: one 1870-hp Mitsubishi MK4R Kasei 23a 14-cylinder radial
Max speed: 587 km/h (365 mph)
Time to height: (J2M3) 6 min 20 sec to 6000 m (19,685 ft)
Service ceiling: 11,700 m (38,385 ft)
Max range: 1899 km (1180 miles)
Wing span: 10.80 m (35 ft 5 in)
Length: 9.95 m (31 ft 10 in)
Height: 3.95 m (12ft 11 in)

Weights: 2460 kg (5423 lb) empty; 3435 kg (7573 lb) loaded
Armament: four wing-mounted 20-mm cannon (reduced to two on later variants)

Mitsubishi A7M
The A7M *Reppu* (Hurricane) was the outcome of a programme, initiated in 1940, for an advanced naval fighter to replace the Zero. The project was delayed by constant problems, particularly in connection with the Nakajima Homare 22 engine that was selected as the type's original powerplant. The prototype A7M1 did not fly until 6 May 1944. It was found to be seriously underpowered, and so the Homare was replaced in the sixth airframe by the Mitsubishi MK9A radial engine. This aircraft became the prototype A7M2, which made its first flight on 13 October 1944.

The project was dogged by misfortune; the Daiko engine plant, responsible for producing the MK9A, was severely damaged by massive B-29 bombing raids, and production facilities at Nagoya were wrecked by a powerful earthquake. The second prototype was destroyed in a landing accident; the first, third and fifth were destroyed by air attack. Only the fourth, sixth and seventh prototypes were airworthy at the end of the war, and only one production aircraft had been completed.

The N1K2-J *Shiden-kai* was an improved version of the *Shiden* with a low-mounted wing, eliminating the need for the long and complex undercarriage of the initial version. It was an excellent fighter, but American bombing of aircraft and engine factories seriously disrupted production plans. This is the prototype N1K2-J. (*Philip Jarrett*)

What the *Reppu* – known to the Allies as 'Sam' – might have achieved had it been produced in quantity earlier was summed up by Saburo Sakai, one of the pilots who test-flew the type.

'All the rumours were true. The *Reppu* was a sensational aircraft, the fastest I had ever flown. It took my breath away with its tremendous speed, and its rate of climb was astounding. With a powerful engine, a four-bladed propeller, and new superchargers, the *Reppu* ran away from everything in the air, Japanese or American. I could fly circles in a climb around either the Hellcat or the Mustang...'

A7M Specification
Powerplant: one 1570-hp Mitsubishi MK9A 18-cylinder radial
Max speed: 627 km/h (390 mph) at 6600 m (21,655 ft)
Time to height: 9 min 54 sec to 6000 m (19,685 ft)
Service ceiling: 10,900 m (35,760 ft)
Wing span: 14.00 m (45 ft 11 in)
Length: 11.00 m (36 ft 1 in)
Height: 4.28 m (14 ft 0 in)
Weights: 3226 kg (7112 lb) empty, 4720 kg (10,406 lb) loaded
Armament: four wing-mounted 20-mm cannon

Kawanishi N1K1-J
Known by the Allied code-name 'George', the *Shiden* (Violet Lightning) was a land-based fighter developed from the *Kyofu* fighter floatplane, known to the Allies as 'Rex'. The original seaplane, which first flew in 1942, was almost as fast and agile as the Zero in spite of the drag from its huge float.

Manufacture of a landplane variant started in August 1943. The *Shiden* was produced in two models, the N1K1-J and the N1K2-J Model 21. The Model 21 had a redesigned airframe that had its wing moved from the mid-fuselage (a feature inherited from the original floatplane design) to a more standard low-wing monoplane configuration. It also featured modified tail surfaces. Both operational models were prominent in the Philippines, around Formosa and in the defence of the Japanese home islands. Production totals were 1098 N1K1-Js and 415 N1K2-Js.

The *Shiden* proved to be one of the finest fighter aircraft to see action in the Pacific Theatre, and was probably the most agile fighter of the war. In the hands of a skilled pilot the *Shiden* was a formidable weapon; in February 1945, for example, the Japanese ace Kaneyoshi Muto engaged 12 US Navy Hellcats single-handed and destroyed four of them, forcing the others to break off combat.

Known to the Allies as 'Oscar', the Nakajima Ki.43 *Hayabusa* (Peregrine Falcon) was the Japanese Army's counterpart of the Navy's Zero, and like the A6M it was in first-line service from the first day of the war until the last. The Ki.43 was also flown by the Royal Thai Air Force during the war. (*Philip Jarrett*)

N1K1 Specification

Powerplant: one 1990-hp Nakajima NK9H Homare 21 18-cylinder radial
Max speed: 581 km/h (361 mph) at 6000 m (19,685 ft)
Service ceiling: 12,500 m (41,010 ft)
Max range: 2544 km (1581 miles)
Wing span: 12.00 m (39 ft 4 in)
Length: 8.88 m (29 ft 1 in)
Height: 4.06 m (13 ft 3 in)
Weights: 2897 kg (6387 lb) empty, 3900 kg (8598 lb) loaded
Armament: two 20-mm cannon in wing leading edges and two in underwing gondolas, plus two 7.7-mm machine-guns in upper forward fuselage.

JAPANESE ARMY FIGHTERS

Nakajima Ki.43

Known as 'Oscar' to the Allies, the Nakajima Ki.43 *Hayabusa* (Peregrine Falcon)was the Japanese Army's counterpart of the Navy's Zero fighter, and like the Zero it was in action from the first day of the Pacific war until the last. Design work on the *Hayabusa* began in 1937. The prototype flew in early January 1939 and was followed by 716 early production models; these were the Ki.43-I, K.43-Ia, Ki.43-Ib and Ki.43-Ic, the last two having a heavier

armament. In 1942 a greatly improved model, the Ki.43-II, made its appearance in three sub-variants, the Ki.43-IIa and -IIb, and the Ki.43-KAI, which adopted all the refinements incorporated in the earlier models. The final model was the Ki.43-III, the only variant to include cannon in its armament.

Production of all versions totalled 5878 aircraft, including 3200 by Nakajima and 2629 by Tachikawa. The *Hayabusa* was the Allies' principal opponent in Burma and was encountered in large numbers during the battle for Leyte, in the Philippines, and in the defence of the Kurile Islands north of Japan. An excellent and versatile fighter in its day, the *Hayabusa*'s main drawback was its lack of adequate armament, and it was hopelessly outclassed by the end of the war.

Ki.43-IIb Specification

Type: fighter-bomber
Powerplant: one 1150-hp Nakajima Ha.115 14-cylinder radial
Max speed: 530 km/h (329 mph) at 5000 m (16,405 ft)
Time to height: 5 min 30 sec to 5000 m (16,405 ft)
Service ceiling: 11,200 m (36,750 ft)
Max range: 3200 km (1990 miles)
Wing span: 35 ft 6 in (10.84 m)

The Nakajima Ki.44 *Shoki* (Devil-Queller), known to the Allies as 'Tojo', first flew in August 1940. The Ki.44 was an effective interceptor with a superb rate of climb, but it was very difficult to fly and landing accidents cost the lives of many inexperienced Japanese pilots. (*Philip Jarrett*)

Length: 29 ft 3 in (8.92 m)
Height: 10 ft 8 in (3.27 m)
Weights: 1910 kg (4211 lb) empty, 2590 kg (5710 lb) loaded
Armament: two 12.7-mm machine-guns in upper forward fuselage; external bomb load of 500 kg (1102lb)

Nakajima Ki.44

First flown in prototype form in August 1940, The Nakajima Ki-44 *Shoki* (Devil-Queller) was designed specifically as an interceptor and proved to be outstanding in this role, due to its excellent speed and rate of climb, which was the highest of any Japanese fighter. It was, however, a dangerous aircraft to fly, especially at low speeds because of its high wing loading, and many inexperienced trainees were killed in landing accidents.

The most effective version of the *Shoki* was the heavily-armed Ki.44-IIc, which was used in the air defence of Japan and achieved some noteworthy successes against the American B-29 bombers. The *Shoki* was also operational in the East Indies, where it defended the Sumatran oilfields. In all, 1225 examples of the

Shoki were built. The type was code-named 'Tojo' by the Allies.

Ki.44 Specification
Type: interceptor
Powerplant: one 1520-hp Nakajima Ha.109 14-cylinder radial
Max speed: 605 km/h (376 mph) at 5000 m (16,405 ft)
Time to height: 4 min 17 sec to 5000 m (16,405 ft)
Service ceiling: 11,200 m (36,745 ft)
Max range: 1702 km (1070 miles)
Wing span: 9.45 m (31 ft)
Length: 8.79 m (28 ft 10 in)
Height: 3.25 m (10 ft 8 in)
Weights: 2106 kg (4643 lb) empty, 2764 kg (6094 lb) loaded
Armament: two nose-mounted and two wing-mounted 12.7-mm machine-guns

Kawasaki Ki.61
Code-named 'Tony' by the Allies, the Kawasaki Ki.61 *Hien* (Swallow)was designed to replace the Nakajima Ki.43 *Hayabusa* in Japanese Army service. Delivered to front-line air units from

Dubbed 'Tony' by the Allies, the Kawasaki Ki.61 was the first Japanese fighter to feature armour protection and self-sealing fuel tanks. Although its wing loading was high, it was well liked by its pilots. Some, like the example seen here, were used by the Chinese Nationalists after the war. (*Harry Holmes*)

The Kawasaki Ki.60, built around the German DB.601A inverted-vee liquid-cooled engine, was designed as a heavy interceptor. The type's performance fell short of expectations and only the three prototypes pictured here were completed. It was abandoned in favour of the lighter Ki.61. (*Harry Holmes*)

The Nakajima Ki.84 *Hayate* (Gale), known to the Allies as 'Frank', was a fine fighting machine which replaced the Ki.44 *Shoki* on the production lines at the end of 1944. The aircraft was mass-produced, and was one of the principal fighters in service with the Japanese Army Air Force at the end of the war. (*Philip Jarrett*)

August 1942, it was the only operational Japanese fighter to feature an inverted-V engine (a licence-built DB 601), and until Allied pilots became familiar with it its appearance gave rise to erroneous reports that the Japanese were using Messerschmitt 109s. In fact, the Bf 109 had been considered for production as the Japanese Army's primary interceptor in 1940, but the *Shoki* was chosen in preference. By the end of the Pacific war 3028 Ki.61s had been built, serving in all areas. The principal versions were the Ki.61-I (1380 aircraft built in two sub-variants, differentiated by their armament); the Ki.61 Kai, with a lengthened fuselage and different armament fits (1274 built); and the Ki.61-II, optimised for high altitude operation with a Kawasaki Ha.140 engine (374 built).

Ki.61-I Specification
Powerplant: one 1175-hp Kawasaki Ha.40 12-cylinder inverted-vee
Max speed: 592 km/h (368 mph) at 5000 m (16,405 ft)
Time to height: 5 min 31 sec to 5000 m (16,405 ft)
Service ceiling: 11,600 m (37,730 ft)
Max range: 1100 km (684 miles)
Wing span: 12.00 m (39 ft 4 in)

Length: 8.75 m (28 ft 8 in)
Height: 3.70 m (12 ft 1 in)
Weights: 2210kg (4872 lb) empty, 2950 kg (6504 lb) loaded
Armament: four 12.7-mm machine-guns, two in upper forward fuselage and two in wings

Nakajima Ki.84
First flown in April 1943, the Ki.84 *Hayate* (Gale), known to the Allies as 'Frank', was more manoeuvrable and easier to handle than the *Shoki*, which it replaced on the production line at the end of 1944. The Ki.84 was mass-produced, about 3500 being completed before the end of hostilities. The type was produced in two principal variants, the Ki.84-I (four sub-variants, each with increasingly powerful armament) and the Ki.84-II, which had a wooden rear fuselage and fittings in an effort to reduce the drain on Japan's dwindling reserves of strategic light alloys. The last version was the Ki.116, a converted Ki.84-Ia with a lighter engine.

Ki.84-I Specification
Powerplant: one 1900-hp Nakajima Ha.45 18-cylinder radial
Max speed: 631 km/h (392 mph) at 5000 m (16,405 ft)

The Kawasaki Ki.100 was essentially a hybrid aircraft, a Ki.61 *Hien* airframe fitted with a Mitsubishi radial engine. It proved to be an excellent combat aircraft, and in the hands of an experienced pilot it represented a serious threat to American fighters over Japan in the closing months of the war. (*Harry Holmes*)

Time to height: 5 min 54 sec to 5000 m (16,405 ft)
Service ceiling: 10,500 m (34,450 ft)
Max range: 2168 km (1347 miles)
Wing span: 11.24 m (36 ft 10 in)
Length: 9.92 m (32 ft 6 in)
Height: 3.39 m (11ft 1 in)
Weights: 2660 kg (5864 lb) empty, 3613 kg (7955 lb) loaded
Armament: two fuselage-mounted 12.7-mm machine-guns and two wing-mounted 20-mm cannon

Kawasaki Ki.100

The Kawasaki Ki.100, which was never allocated a code-name by the Allies, was a Ki.61 airframe fitted with a radial engine, the licence-built DB.601 being in short supply. As these engines had proved to be unreliable in any case, it was decided to fit the airframes with the 1500-hp Mitsubishi Ha.112-II radial.

The 'new' aircraft flew for the first time on 1 February 1945 and proved to handle superbly. Conversion of 275 Ki.61-II airframes began immediately. The Ki.100 was produced in two principal series, the Ia and Ib, the latter being new-build aircraft; 396 examples of both versions were completed before production was halted in August, just before the end of the war. The Ki.100 showed itself to be very effective in low- and medium-altitude combat against Hellcats and Mustangs, but it was less suited to engaging B-29s at high altitude. It saw a great amount of action over Japan in the closing months of the war.

Ki.100 Specification
Powerplant: one 1500-hp Mitsubishi Ha.112-II 14-cylinder radial
Max speed: 580 km/h (360 mph) at 5000 m (16,405 ft)
Time to height: 6 min to 5000 m (16,405 ft)
Service ceiling: 11,000 m (36,090 ft)
Max range: 2000 km (1242 miles)
Wing span: 12.00 m (39 ft 4 in)
Length: 8.82 m (28 ft 11 in)
Height: 3.75 m (12 ft 3 in)
Weights: 2525 kg (5567 lb) empty, 3495 kg (7705 lb) loaded
Armament: two 20-mm cannon in upper forward fuselage and two 12.7-mm (0.50-in) machine-guns in wings.

Appendix 1
Technical Descriptions

Fuselage

The Mitsubishi A6M Zero was a single-seat carrier-borne fighter of all-metal construction, with fabric-covered control surfaces. The fuselage was of semi-monocoque duralumin construction with light alloy (Extra-Super Dualumin) covering built in two sections. The forward section, built as an integral part of the wing centre section, included the engine mounting, the fuselage fuel tank, the oil tank, the cockpit area and a radio compartment aft of the cockpit (this was used as a stowage space in the A6M2; radios were first installed in the A6M3). The rear section of the fuselage was detachable, extending from a splice frame located just aft of the wing trailing edge. It provided attachments for the tail surfaces, inflatable flotation bag, arrester hook and tail wheel. The vertical stabliser (tail fin) was an integral part of the rear fuselage.

Wings

The all-metal two-spar wings were of high aspect ratio with pronounced taper, ending at rounded tips (except in the case of the A6M3, which had squared-off tips). The selected aerofoil was the Mitsubishi No.118, developed from the tried and tested B-9 and NACA 23012 series. At 30 per cent chord the dihedral was 5°40' and the angle of incidence changed from 2° at the root to 0.5° at the tip. To prevent wingtip stalls a 'washout' was applied from the centre part of the wing towards the tip, gradually increasing the camber near the wingtips. Provision was made for the wings to accommodate two 20-mm cannon (one in each wing), four fuel tanks, two inflatable flotation bags, and main wheel wells. Metal split flaps with a width of 1.8 m (5 ft 11 in) were located between the ailerons and wing root fairings. The fabric-covered ailerons, of smaller chord than the flaps, were fitted with metal trim tabs (adjustable only on the ground) and a large external balance weight. The pitot tube was situated near the tip of the port wing. To facilitate handling and stowage aboard aircraft carriers, 50 cm (1 ft 7 in) of each wingtip folded upwards (A6M2 only).

Tail

The tail unit was of all-metal construction except for the rudder and elevators, which were fabric-covered. The tail fin formed an integral part with the rear fuselage, while the horizontal tail surfaces were attached just above the fuselage centreline.

Each elevator had a metal trim tab that could be controlled by the pilot, but the rudder trim tab could only be adjusted on the ground.

Undercarriage

The undercarriage was hydraulically operated and fully retractable. The main wheels retracted inwards into wells situated forward of the front spar, and when raised were enclosed by fairing plates which fitted flush with the lower wing surfaces. The tail wheel was also fully retractable into the tail cone, but had no fairing doors. An arrester hook was recessed into the lower rear fuselage.

Cockpit

The cockpit was of conventional layout, with a standard instrument panel and a Type 98 reflector gunsight. The breeches of the two nose-mounted 7.7-mm machine-guns protruded into the cockpit, the trigger and gun selector switch being mounted on the throttle. The A6M2 Zero did not carry R/T equipment, but the A6M3 and successive aircraft were fitted with a Japanese Type 96 Ku 1 high frequency transmitter/receiver which had an effective transmitting range of 80 km (50 miles) at 3050 m (10,000 ft). A Type 1 Ku 3 radio compass was fitted, with the antenna loop just behind the cockpit. The oxygen system was supplied by two bottles installed in the rear fuselage.

Powerplants

The prototype A6M1 was powered by a Mitsubishi Zuisei 13 engine. The Zuisei (Holy Star) was a 14-cylinder air-cooled radial driving a three-blade metal propeller. It was rated at 780 hp for take-off and 950 hp at 4200 m (13,780 ft).

The first production fighter, the A6M2, was powered by a Nakajima NK1C Sakae 12. The Sakae (Prosperity) was a 14-cylinder air-cooled radial rated at 940 hp for take-off and 950 hp at 4200m (13,780 ft). It drove a three-blade metal propeller.

Variants from the A6M3 to the A6M5c were powered by the Nakajima NK1F Sakae 21. The upgraded 14-cylinder radial was rated at 1130 hp for take-off, 1100 hp at 2850 m (9350 ft) and 980 hp at 6000 m (19,685 ft). The engine drove a three-blade, constant-speed Sumitomo metal propeller.

Later A6M5cs and the A6M7 used one Nakajima Sakae 31 14-cylinder air-cooled radial, rated at 1130 hp for take-off, 1100 hp at 2850 m (9350 ft) and 980 hp at 6000 m (19,685 ft).

The final A6M8 variant was powered by one Mitsubishi MK8P Kinsei 62. The Kinsei (Golden Star) was a 14-cylinder radial, rated at 1560 hp for take-off, 1340 hp at 2100 m (6890ft) and 1180 hp at 5800 m (19,030 ft). It drove a three-blade, constant-speed Sumitomo metal propeller.

Fuel system

(data refers to A6M3)

One 60-litre (13.2-Imp gal) fuselage fuel tank located between the oil tank and the instrument panel; two 210-litre (46.2-Imp gal) fuel tanks located in the wings adjacent to the wing roots; two 45-litre (9.9-Imp gal) fuel tanks located between the wing spars outboard of the cannon; one 330-litre (72.6-Imp gal) ventral drop tank fabricated from light alloy or plywood. The oil tank, situated in the forward fuselage, held 65 litres (14.3 Imp gal).

Camouflage and markings

Until mid-1942, most Zeros were painted in non-specular sky grey overall with the exception of the engine cowling, which was usually painted black. The only other markings were the red and white national insignia on wings and fuselage, unit markings on the vertical tail surfaces (normally in red), and bands of varying colours around the rear fuselage, which were used to identify those aircraft which belonged to group or flight leaders.

When operations in the Philippines and Solomons revealed the need for some form of camouflage, dark green blotches were applied to the upper surfaces. From 1943, a standard scheme of dark green upper surfaces and light grey under surfaces was adopted, the engine cowling remaining black. Any unit tail markings were now in white.

Appendix 2
Weapons

Cannon

The Mitsubishi Zero was armed with the 20-mm Type 99 cannon, which was the standard aircraft cannon of the Imperial Japanese Navy. The Type 99 was a licence-produced version of the Swiss Oerlikon 20-mm cannon, which was also installed in a number of European fighter aircraft.

A principal reason behind the selection of this weapon was that although it had a low muzzle velocity, it was light and sufficiently compact to allow installation in the Zero's aerodynamically clean wing. It also fired explosive shells. The cannon was mass-produced under licence in Japan by the Dai-Nihon Heiki Company Ltd.

The Type 99 Model 1 Mk 3, installed in the A6M1 and A6M2, used drum magazines, while the later Model 2 Mk 4 was belt-fed. The Type 99 was constantly modified during its operational life, its length and weight undergoing several changes. For example, the length of the Model 1 was 1.332 m (52 inches), increasing to 1.890 m (74 inches) in the Model 2 Mk 4.

The rate of fire ranged from 490 rounds per minute (Model 2 Mk 3) to 750 rpm (Model 2 Mk 5). Muzzle velocities ranged from 1970 ft/sec in the Model 1 up to 2490 ft/sec in the Model 2 Mk 5. Effective range for early guns was 800 m (2625 ft); later weapons were effective out to 1000 m (3280 ft).

An enlarged version of the 20-mm Type 99, the 30-mm Type 5, which was fed from 42-round magazines, was entering service at the war's end.

Machine-guns

The Zero's original machine-gun armament consisted of two nose-mounted 7.7-mm (0.303-in) Type 97 machine-guns. The rifle calibre Type 97 was replaced in later variants of the A6M by the 13.2-mm (0.51-in) Type 3 belt-fed heavy machine-gun.

Specification
Type 99 Model 2 Mk 4 cannon
Calibre: 20 mm
Length of gun: 1.890 m (6 ft 2 in)
Weight: 37.57 kg (82.65 lb)
Rate of fire: 550 rounds per minute
Muzzle velocity: 600 m/sec (1970 ft/sec)
Ammo feed: belt feed, 125 rounds per gun
Weight of shell: 123 g (0.246 lb)

Specification
Type 97 machine-gun
Calibre: 7.7 mm (0.303 in)
Length: 1.04 m (41 in)
Weight: 11.79 kg (26 lb)
Rate of fire: 1000 rounds per minute
Muzzle velocity: 750 m/sec (2460 ft/sec)
Effective range: 600 m (1970 ft)
Ammunition: 500 rounds per gun

Specification
Type 3 heavy machine-gun
Calibre: 13.2 mm (0.52 in)
Length: 1.55 m (61 in)
Weight: 29.94 kg (66 lb)
Rate of fire: 800 rounds per minute
Muzzle velocity: 790 m/sec (2590 ft/sec)
Effective range: 900 m (2950 ft)
Ammunition: 450 rounds per gun

External stores

Normal: two 60-kg (132-lb) bombs
Maximum: (A6M7/8) one 500-kg (1102-lb) bomb
Kamikaze: one 250-kg (550-lb) bomb
Air-to-air: (A6M6c and A6M8) eight 10-kg (22-lb) or two 60-kg (132-lb) rockets
Drop tanks: (A6M1 to A6M6) one 330-litre (72.6-Imp gal); (A6M7/8) two 350-litre (77-Imp gal)

Appendix 3
Zero Production

Because of the immense destruction caused by USAAF bombing of the Japanese aviation industry, no records survive to give an accurate breakdown of production for the various sub-series of the A6M.

	Mitsubishi	Nakajima	Total
Mar 1939 to Mar 1942	722	115	837
Apr 1942 to Mar 1943	729	960	1689
Apr 1943 to Mar 1944	1164	2268	3432
Apr 1944 to Mar 1945	1145	2342	3487
Apr 1945 to Aug 1945	119	885	1004
Total production	**3879**	**6570**	**10,449**

Although the A6M was a Mitsubishi design, the rival company Nakajima built almost twice as many fighters as the original manufacturer.

Appendix 4
Zero Units

Units which flew the Zero, showing unit tail codes where known or appropriate

Carrier-borne

Unit	Tail code	Unit	Tail code
Akagi Fighter Squadron	AI	*Zuikaku* Fighter Squadron	EII
Kaga Fighter Squadron	VI		(AII late 1943)
	(All Apr–June 1942)	*Zuiho* Fighter Squadron	EIII
Ryujo Fighter Squadron	DI		(AIII late 1943)
Soryu Fighter Squadron	B1	*Shoho* Fighter Squadron	DII (Sept 1941–May 1942)
Hiryu Fighter Squadron	BII	*Junyo* Fighter Squadro	DII (May–Sept 1942)
Shokaku Fighter Squadron	EI	*Hiyo* Fighter Squadron	DI
	(AI late 1943)		

Land-based

Unit	Tail code	Unit	Tail code
2nd Air Group	Q, T3	Air Group 254	54, 254
3rd Air Group	X	Air Group 256	256
4th Air Group	F	Air Group 261	61
6th Air Group	U	Air Group 263	63
12th Air Group	3 (1937–Sept 1941)	Air Group 265	65
14th Air Group	9	Air Group 281	81
Chitose Air Group	S	Air Group 301	01
Tainan Air Group	V	Air Group 302	3D
Air Group 131	131	Air Group 331	31, 331
Air Group 201	WI/OI	Air Group 332	32
Air Group 202	O2, X2,	Air Group 341	341
	301 (March–July 1944)	Air Group 343	43
Air Group 203	03, 203	Air Group 352	352
Air Group 204	T2	Air Group 381	381
Air Group 205	205	Air Group 601	311/312/313,
Air Group 221	21, 221		601 (1945)
Air Group 251	U1	Air Group 634	634
Air Group 252	G, Y2	Air Group 652	652, 321
	252 (June 1943–Feb 1944)	Air Group 653	331/332/333,
Air Group 253	K, U3		653 (1944)
	53 (Sept 1943–Dec 1944)	Air Group 721	'Jin' (Japanese for 'God')

Appendix 5
Museum Aircraft and Survivors

An airworthy example of an A6M Zero, powered by the original Nakajima Sakae engine, is maintained by the Museum of Flying, Santa Monica, California. In 1990, the museum took delivery of the crated remains of three more Zeros, recovered from the Pacific island of Babo, near the western tip of New Guinea. The aircraft, together with a G4M 'Betty' bomber, had been put out of action during a US air attack. Several Nakajima Sakae engines were also recovered, and on examination one of them was found to contain oil, a good sign for future restoration.

The restorers selected the most complete Zero and spread it out on the floor of the restoration hangar. A close look told them that the road to full restoration would be long and difficult; the airframe was heavily corroded and many components were missing. A full inventory of all the parts was made, and work began on restoring the tail section and rear fuselage. The latter was virtually complete when the restoration team, under the direction of Bruce Lockwood, received an unexpected windfall; a Japanese visitor handed over a complete set of Zero blueprints, carefully preserved since World War II.

Despite this, work progressed painfully slowly, as the Museum of Flying's personnel were also working on other restoration projects. It was therefore decided to ship the Zero and all associated parts to Russia, where work would be carried on by employees of the Yakovlev Company. The details were arranged through Flight Magic, a Santa Monica-based firm specializing in restoration work and the production of vintage aircraft.

The Zero's airframe, virtually complete, returned to the USA in 1996 and went to Fighter Rebuilders at Chino for engine installation. The selected powerplant was the Pratt & Whitney R-1820 radial, chosen for its reliability, while the Russians persevered with the task of restoring a Sakae engine to full working order.

On 16 April 1998, the restored Zero took to the air for the first time, with Steve Hinton of Fighter Rebuilders at the controls. The aircraft carries the American civil registration N6582L, and the tail code X-133, representing an A6M2 of the 3rd Air Group Fighter Squadron.

Appendix 6
Zero Models

The following A6M Zero model kits are available on the international market.

Hasegawa
A6M2 Type 21 (1/72nd)
A6M5 Type 52 (1/72nd)
A6M5e Type 52 (1/72nd)

A6M2 Type 11 (1/48th)
A6M2b Type 21 (1/48th)
A6M5e Type 52 (1/48th)

Revell
A6M5 (1/32nd)

Tamiya
A6M2 Type 21 (1/48th)
A6M3 Type 32 (1/48th)
A6M5c Type 52 (1/48th)

'Collectable' Zeros include the Corgi Aviation Archive's A6M2 Model 21, representing the aircraft flown by Japanese ace Saburo Sakai.

To commemorate the 60th anniversary of the attack on Pearl Harbor, Diverse Images produced a pair of hand-crafted 1/72nd scale pewter models, one a Curtiss P-40C Warhawk and the other a Mitsubishi A6M2 Zero, mounted on a diorama which includes a stainless steel plaque featuring a map of Oahu, the Hawaiian island on which Pearl Harbor is situated. This was a limited edition of 60 examples.

The aircraft were also available separately, as limited editions of 500, the P-40 representing one of the aircraft that managed to take off from Bellows Field on the day of the attack and the Zero representing the lead fighter from the carrier *Akagi*.

Zero kit details supplied by
Windsock Models, 5-7 Fore Bondgate, Bishop Auckland, Co Durham DL14 7PF (01388 609766)

Appendix 7
Zero Books

Bueschel, R.M.
Mitsubishi A6M1/2/2N Zero-Sen in Japanese Naval Air Service.
Osprey/Aircam No. 16 (Vol 1), 1970

Hata, I and Yasuho, I.
Japanese Naval Aces and Fighter Units in World War II.
Airlife, 1989

Horikoshi, J.
Eagles of Mitsubishi: the Story of the Zero Fighter.
Washington U.P., 1992

Mikesh R.C. and Watanabe, R.
Zero Fighter.
Jane's Aircraft Spectacular, 1981

Mikesh, R.C.
Zero.
Motorbooks International, 1994

Sakai, S. (With Martin Caidin and Fred Saito)
Samurai!
William Kimber, 1959

Index

Page numbers in *italics* refer to illustrations.